JAZZ WORKS
for ensembles

Teacher's Book & CD

1. initial level

by Jeremy Price & Mike Sheppard

THE ASSOCIATED BOARD OF THE ROYAL SCHOOLS OF MUSIC

First published in 1999 by
The Associated Board of the Royal Schools of Music (Publishing) Limited
14 Bedford Square, London WC1B 3JG, United Kingdom
www.abrsmpublishing.co.uk

© 1999 by The Associated Board of the Royal Schools of Music

All rights reserved. No part of this publication may be reproduced, stored in a retrieval system, or transmitted in any form or by any means, electronic, mechanical, photocopying, recording, or otherwise, without the prior permission of the copyright owner

Written by Jeremy Price and Mike Sheppard
Music editorial and project management by Artemis Music Limited
Design concept by Space DPS Limited
Printed in the United Kingdom by Caligraving Limited, Thetford, Norfolk

A note about the parts:
Wherever possible the instrumental parts have been organised in the same sequence as the Scores, Performance Notes, Teacher's Books and CDs. It should be noted, however, that the sequence of some of the parts has been adjusted to avoid unnecessary and awkward page turns.

Introduction   4

PART ONE - GENERAL

Chapter 1: Improvisation   11
Chapter 2: A step-by-step survival guide for teachers   14
Chapter 3: How to direct a jazz ensemble   17
Chapter 4: How to rehearse a solo section   25
Chapter 5: How to rehearse the ensemble section   29
Chapter 6: Jazz conventions/focus topics   33

PART TWO - THE PIECES

Art's Groove   46
Azul   50
Bear Cave Blues   53
Blue Panther   58
Brecon Beacon   62
Night Run   66
Slice and Dice   69
Straw Boss   72

Glossary   75
Chord Chart   77
Discography   78
On the CD   79
Index   80

Introduction

Welcome to Jazz Works, a specially-commissioned collection of new works for flexible jazz ensemble. These works – scores, parts and accompanying Performance Notes and Teacher's Books – provide you, the teacher or ensemble leader, with all the music, information, training, support materials and advice that you will need to become a polished band leader.

The music has been written with you in mind, whether you are an experienced jazz musician, or a classically-trained (and therefore probably slightly nervous of jazz and improvising) music teacher. In this book you will find a step-by-step guide to all aspects of running a jazz ensemble, from selecting the players, through counting in the band, rehearsing, directing performance and much, much more.

Because a large part of learning to play jazz consists of assimilating its style and musical language, we have recorded a CD of performances of each piece by a professional jazz ensemble. To make our situation as much like yours as we can, we have taken a flexible approach to our own instrumentation. We recognise that in an educational environment the players available to you will vary. Therefore the instrumentation on the CD varies from piece to piece. It is important to remember that this series, like all true jazz pieces, is simply a flexible musical resource for you to use in any way you choose.

For most teachers with little experience of jazz the biggest fear arises out of how to approach improvising, and this is addressed at length in this series. Not only do the pieces at the initial and intermediate levels have specially-constructed, simple chord sequences for novices, but also scale choices are given in the soloing parts. So there will never be a time when either player or teacher does not have some suitable options to hand. You might like to think of this as analogous to the stabilising wheels a child has when learning to ride a bike. The analogy is a good one because, by the time you get to the advanced level the scale choices are removed and by this stage both player and leader will have accrued enough knowledge either to know the relevant scales or to be able to work them out.

This set of eight initial level pieces is designed to provide an introduction to jazz music and to encourage and enable young musicians in their first explorations of jazz improvisation. It is aimed at players of instrumental ability roughly between grades 3 and 4, though it is in the nature of jazz that some things may be asked of the players that takes them beyond this ability range.

Modular compositions

The pieces are organised in a modular fashion – we provide you with the building blocks and you construct the building! So, we give you intros, heads (main tunes), interludes, open solo sections and codas, and you decide in which order they should be played. This may be a new way of working for you, but this freedom to create using the basic resource lies at the heart of the jazz musician's approach.

So, while every piece is set out in the score and parts in a workable format, experimentation with the structure is very much encouraged. The form is also adaptable, allowing each piece to be tailored to the group's needs. The form diagram for each piece in the Performance Notes suggests ways in which this can be done.

The modular nature of the compositions is dual purpose. Firstly, it demands that the group must decide upon the exact content of the performance for themselves. This helps capture the essence of jazz performance practice in that it promotes a high degree of personal involvement and ownership of the music. Secondly, it enables the group to work with the piece at a level most suited to them. Virtually all the pieces can be abridged in order to simplify them, or extended once the performers feel more comfortable with the material.

The jazz composer

Jazz music, despite being essentially an improvised music, nearly always involves an element of composed material. The proportions of the improvised and composed elements can vary tremendously from a free improvisation based on a theme to a fully-orchestrated piece with just a short solo in the middle. The composer writing for jazz musicians must decide upon this balance and also realise that the greater the degree of improvising space provided, the greater the responsibility he or she is giving over to the performers.

The task of the jazz composer is essentially to create a space within which musicians can improvise. These eight pieces are written to provide this space and can be viewed as vehicles for the performer's own ideas and improvisations. The composers have given the performers a significant amount of responsibility in giving them many opportunities to shape the piece to their own needs.

Standard terms and conventions

The beauty of jazz is that it is largely an aural tradition, and as such it resists attempts at pinning labels on it. Naming styles, chords, scales or sections of the music (like head, B section and so on) usually manages either to alienate, confuse or annoy one or another section of the jazz community.

Jazz is an art form, so any didactic approach to teaching it is rightly met with suspicion – as educators we must aim for an inclusive approach that is neither judgemental nor blinkered in the way it deals with educational methodology. There are many traditions within what we broadly refer to as jazz, encompassing a wide range of styles and cultures. It is vital to understand the multi-ethnic provenance of jazz, and to celebrate that diversity in all efforts to educate and enlighten.

All musical notation is merely a representation of the musical sounds the composer intends. It is up to the musician to bring the printed page to life through his or her own interpretation. To arrive at this interpretation the musician will call upon his or her experiences of music, either as a listener or as a performer, and assimilate them into a unique performance style. This is true of all forms of music, but is especially true of jazz.

Jazz music has evolved aurally because its principal means of communication is via performance or, more significantly these days, via recordings. If you want to become familiar with the work of a certain artist in jazz, you do not go and buy a book of sheet music; you go to one of their gigs or buy a recording by them, or both.

If you have ever tried transcribing an improvised solo it will soon become apparent how inadequate music notation is. You can notate pitch and rhythm to a certain extent, but if the player is bending notes and pulling the tempo around, or using a variety of quaver feels combined with other jazz techniques, you will soon realise that your transcription is a mere representation of only some of what is happening. The transcription will be useful if you have the recording as well, but on its own will probably be less than half the story.

We now understand that there are certain nuances and elements of style in jazz that appear clumsy on the page, or are even impossible to notate. So what bearing does this have on our interpretation of written music in the jazz idiom? The answer is that whenever you play written music you have to contribute the style, nuance and inflection yourself. This will come from your own experience of jazz, so the more you listen, the better you will become. However, this book will be useless if it fails to communicate certain key principles, and in order to communicate effectively we must strive for a common understanding of what we are saying and trying to achieve.

How do you teach jazz?

This is another thorny question. Some musicians like to take a natural approach while others are more studied. There are many, many ways of learning how to improvise, and we offer a number of approaches that teachers with classical music experience should be able to understand quite easily.

However, while we go to great lengths to equip you with the knowledge you will need to become an effective teacher and advocate of jazz, we would urge you not to become a slavish adherent to any one system. For example, in teaching the twelve-bar blues we explain three methods of generating material for solos (blues scale, guide tones and scale choices based on the moving harmony), but these are not the only choices available to you.

These will undoubtedly give you a core vocabulary and an understanding of how jazz harmony works, but you should also search elsewhere for inspiration. If everybody used the same resources in the same way, all jazz would sound more or less the same. The reason it does not is that good jazz musicians take these basic tools and use them as a point of departure, creating music that is palpably and demonstrably their own.

That is why a West Coast blues band sounds so different from an African Township group. It is why Jan Garbarek sounds so different from Sonny Rollins; it is why one note from Miles Davis can send shivers down your spine; it explains how a flu-ridden pianist playing an out-of-tune piano held an audience spellbound for an entire evening whilst creating one of the biggest selling jazz albums of all time (Keith Jarrett in the Köln Concert).

Once you have an understanding of how jazz works, you will have a resource that will inform and inspire all your music-making and listening. You will become a better all-round musician, with many of the skills and techniques you use in jazz being transferable to other disciplines.

Part One −
General

Chapter 1: Improvisation

What exactly is improvisation? This whole book is primarily concerned with improvisation, so let us take a moment to talk about what this word means. There is a great deal of mythology surrounding improvising, so much so that it has almost become one of the mystical arts of music practice. Consider these two fictional jazz characters: on the one hand there is the musician who says things like, 'Oh, I just hear the notes and blow!', and then there is the other kind who will blind you with science: '…I love this scale, that flat-nine, sharp-five, altered extended dominant structure with the demented 11th is such a beautiful colour…'.

There will always be romantics, and there will always be 'anoraks'. Remember, jazz theory and performance is a logical and learnable process. No musician works in isolation, and this is particularly true of the jazz musician. Whether or not they are aware of it, our two fictional jazzers both come from pretty much the same background, and have gone through similar learning processes. They will have learned to play their instruments, firstly acquiring the technical facility to enable them to approach jazz. Then they will have been exposed to other people's music, which they assimilated, either through a conscious effort of learning, or by absorbing it through repeated exposure.

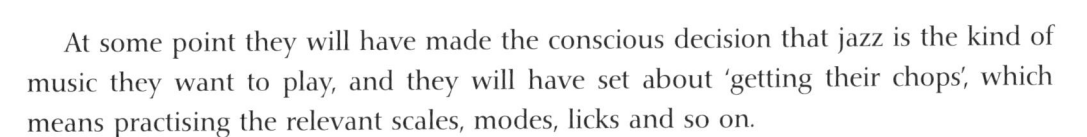

At some point they will have made the conscious decision that jazz is the kind of music they want to play, and they will have set about 'getting their chops', which means practising the relevant scales, modes, licks and so on.

Jazz musicians borrow heavily from one another, so much so that it has become a kind of game for one musician to quote another in his soloing. This is an extension of the simple learning process whereby a novice musician takes landmark recordings, works out the chord sequence (or looks it up in any one of a number of source books that are readily available) and listens carefully to what an experienced player has done with it, often borrowing licks for his or her own solos. Many musicians take this so far as to transcribe the solos of their heroes, lovingly notating every subtle inflection and nuance.

So, there is an established route from absolute beginner to fledgling jazz soloist. But what about you and your pupils? Where do you start?

If you are worried whether or not you can improvise you will be relieved to know that you already do it all the time. In everyday life there are situations constantly occurring that we have to react to in the moment that they happen. These situations can be as mundane as making a cup of tea in the morning, or making a spontaneous decision at work or school. In both cases you are reacting to circumstances in real time and coming up with a solution.

Another parallel, and probably the most relevant to music, is that of speech. Think of the improvisatory nature of day to day speech. Somebody says something to you,

you hear it and understand the meaning, and without a second thought you can throw back a coherent reply. You can do this because with that person you share a language and common experiences that lend meaning to your communication.

There are words and phrases you both know, and you have an agreed system of rules and grammar to help you organise them. There are also many different levels on which you can communicate. You can talk slang or the Queen's English, the relaxed and vernacular or the precise and formal. Either way you are improvising with speech in real time, in the moment, and it is a fundamental part of human life.

So, you now realise that you are already a supremely gifted improviser. But can you improvise with music? At this stage you probably have a high level of competence on your instrument and a love of, or at least a curiosity about, jazz music.

At first the mass of chord symbols, many with add-ons and extensions, can be confusing and, frankly, a little off-putting to the uninitiated. But remember, learning the language of jazz is like learning any other language – it takes time to achieve anything like fluency.

As with any new subject the first thing you need is a frame of reference – just one thing. That one thing might be a blues scale (just six notes), or it might be a riff that you know works over a dominant 7th. It does not matter what it is, but once you have it, you have a starting point for your journey.

This series is packed full of just such little milestones, and it gives you the theory behind how things work.

You will very quickly pick up some musical vocabulary in the form of phrases and scale choices, some grammar in the form of cadences and stock musical devices, and some shared musical experiences, both through recommended listening and through playing these pieces together. These are the first steps in learning the language of jazz.

The beginner improviser

Making your first acquaintance with improvised music can be a daunting prospect. There are a number of barriers to be overcome. Here is a selection of typical questions that a novice improviser is likely to come up with, along with our answers and solutions.

Q: I've never played a solo in front of my peers or an audience before, let alone one I've got to make up myself. How do I overcome my inhibitions?

A: Inhibitions can be broken down by a deliberate injection of self confidence, and an awareness in the group that this is a new musical language for everyone. Foster an air of mutual self-support and encouragement. Finally, take the plunge – it'll be cold at first but you'll get used to it! This book will look at ways of creating an environment where everyone feels they can get involved.

Q: How do I know which notes are going to sound good? What happens if I play a wrong note or something that sounds horrible?

A: A large part of this book will be about discovering the melodic properties of chord symbols and how to interpret them. In addition to that there will be a wealth of 'safe' source material in the pieces (in the form of written material you can borrow from, and scale choices written out over the relevant chord symbols).

Q: The rhythmic element is obviously very strong in this music. How do I get involved and how can I contribute?

A: Groove and rhythmic drive are essential elements to jazz. We'll be looking at ways of getting everyone responding to the pulse in a musical way, through workshop ideas and group activities. Many of these present great ways to break down inhibitions.

Q: Once I've found the notes that sound good, how will I know what to do with them?

A: By learning to understand how music is constructed. We'll be looking at how to build small phrase structures through simple call-and-response themes and basic motifs. We'll also be looking at how the composed material in the pieces can be used as a starting point for developing vocabulary and melodic ideas.

Q: How do I know when to start playing and when to stop?

A: By learning about form and how music is structured. We'll be looking at how to hear the form, particularly the 'corners' of the music (those parts of the sequence where there is a defining movement or event). We'll be showing how, on the one hand the rhythm section, and on the other hand the episodes of composed music, both serve to outline the structure, and how you can use them as landmarks to keep your bearings.

Chapter 2: A step-by-step survival guide for teachers

For many music teachers, leading a jazz band will be a new experience. Whilst the confidence you have gained from leading other ensembles will stand you in good stead, it might be useful to map out how a typical rehearsal might go. There follows a basic 'lesson plan' for how to approach the first rehearsal, in the form of a step-by-step guide.

Preliminary

1. Consider the resources available to you. This will include personnel, equipment, rehearsal time and space.

2. Select a piece and decide from the performance notes how the instruments at your disposal can be best used. Is there a particular member of the group you wish to feature, or involve in a specific capacity? You may have a particularly strong player who could carry the lead line or do the main soloing.

3. Familiarise yourself with the style of the piece and get to know the main themes and the outline of the harmony.

In rehearsal

4. Arrange the group so that all members have good eye contact with the director and the other performers. Here is a diagram of how we arranged the eight-piece ensemble at the recording session.

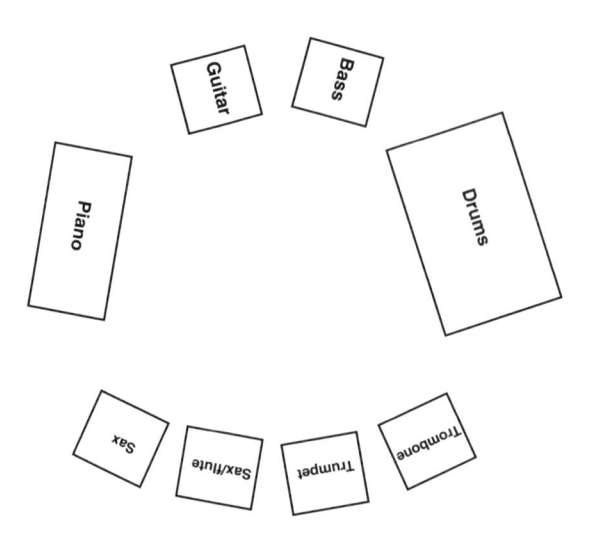

5. Make sure the players know which parts they are playing, especially the front line. If resources allow, parts may be divided into melody lines and accompanying parts.

6. Start by rehearsing a small passage with the rhythm section only (see notes and guidelines on how to rehearse the rhythm section). This will set the tempo and style of the whole piece and give the other performers a strong idea of how their parts will work. The groove and feel will have to be right first before the ensemble material can be added.

7. Decide which part of the piece you want to start rehearsing. It is not always the best idea to start at the very top of the piece. Try rehearsing those players who play the main theme first. This may be a considerable way into the piece, after a lengthy introduction, but the main theme will reveal the identity of the piece and allow the group to get a good grasp of the 'meat' of the composition. Quite often the solo section will be based on the same form as the main theme, so identifying this part of the composition will be a useful aid in understanding the form.

8. Identify one of the solo sections. The comping will have to be of a certain standard before solos can be attempted. Allow the rhythm section to get comfortable with it on their own – ask the other members of the group to follow through their chord changes while you are doing this – and rehearse them until the groove is steady and feels comfortable.

9. Now ask the rhythm section to mark out the form by the use of appropriate fills and varied dynamics. Check that the harmonic content is correct by advising on the chord voicings.

10. Ask for some volunteer soloists or pick someone who needs encouragement. Have the rhythm section play the solo form once through and then invite a soloist to play. Make sure these first attempts are greeted by the whole group with support and encouragement. Gradually add more soloists until you have a number of willing participants.

You now have the basis of a performance. You have not dealt with the piece in its entirety, but you have a solid rhythm section, a good rendition of the main theme and some willing soloists. You are in a position to build and develop the piece on all fronts.

You now have the choice of developing either the ensemble material or the soloing.

Ensemble material

11. Work on the counter-themes or the accompanying lines (remember, you have already rehearsed the main theme). Gradually build them up to a workable level and then combine them with the main theme.

12. Try some backings for the solo sections. Make it clear that these will only be played on your direction. Have the rhythm section play the solo section and choose a soloist. After two choruses cue in the backings, making sure you have good eye

contact with all the members of the band, and that you give a clear and decisive cue in plenty of time.

13. Work on the introduction. It is important that this becomes familiar enough that it 'sits' well every time you play it. It is the first thing the audience hears in the concert, and it is a vital confidence builder for the players. If a piece starts well it will continue well. If it starts badly it will be an uphill struggle to get it back on track. When the band is playing the intro well, practise putting it at the front of the head. Play a few bars into the head before stopping the band, making sure they understand the relationship between intro and head. When everything is to your satisfaction, allow the band to continue through the head in its entirety.

14. Some pieces involve an interlude that may be inserted at any point. Rehearse this in isolation and devise a signal that the group recognises to bring them in and out of this section. Practise this in context, using it in a variety of places throughout the score. Always allow the players to play through into the next section before stopping the band. Although the pieces are modular, with various interlocking and moveable sections, the music should always sound unified, with a sense of organic progression from one section to the next.

15. The end of the piece is extremely important. Many a promising performance has fizzled out because the players were unsure about who was doing what at the end. Avoid this by rehearsing a definite ending and making sure that all your players know what is happening. Decide on how you will end the piece (there may be a choice of codas). Rehearse it and then practise an ending, perhaps by playing the head for the last time, going to the coda. This may need a specific cue from the director.

Solo section

16. Get the rhythm section to play through the solo section to remind everyone of the sound of it, asking the players to follow the sequence through on their own parts.

17. Talk about the form and overall length. Ask the rhythm section to mark out this form, making the rest of the group aware of how they are doing it, and why.

18. Talk about harmony. Most pieces at this level will have some simple melodic properties written out below the chord symbol. It will be either a scale or a simple motif. For more in-depth information on this topic look at the chapter in this book on the solo sections. There you will find specific exercises related to each piece which provide some basic starting points and practice hints, as well as a detailed analysis of what is actually happening, both harmonically and structurally.

19. Once starting points have been discussed and practised, have various individuals solo, and then invite direct feedback from the group. Aim to raise awareness of which were successful approaches and which were less successful.

Now run the whole piece.

Chapter 3: How to direct a jazz ensemble

Directing a jazz ensemble is quite a different thing from conducting an orchestra or wind band. There are certain fundamental differences in the way that jazz music operates that will require a modified approach to conducting.

Firstly, there is a rhythm section. This is the actual centre of what is happening. The rhythm section leads the group in terms of tempo, style and form. Once the rhythm section is playing there is no need to indicate every beat, as do conductors of orchestras. As far as style is concerned everyone should be phrasing according to the type of groove laid down by the rhythm section, so there is little opportunity to shape things in performance. The rhythm section is also responsible for marking out the form, so that job is taken care of too.

Secondly, let us consider the soloists. What the soloists are doing is playing their own ideas and making their own musical decisions 'off the cuff'. The listener wants to hear what this individual has to offer, not what the conductor thinks he should be doing.

So what is left for the director of a jazz ensemble to do? Is he or she entirely redundant? Some jazz musicians would argue that a director is completely superfluous as the few group decisions that need to be made can be taken care of by one or other of the musicians. In fact it is very rare for a jazz group to have someone whose only role is to direct the band.

All the important big band leaders such as Tommy Dorsey, Benny Goodman, Woody Herman and Harry James had important roles to play as instrumental soloists as well as directors. We have all seen the cliché dance bandleader, standing at the front of the band in a white DJ conducting the musicians through a foxtrot that they have played thousands of times before. This is obviously for visual effect, to convince the audience that he is in control rather than for any practical reason.

However, we must of course remember that the requirements for inexperienced musicians at an educational level are different from those of the professional jazz musician. We must also look at the role of the director in rehearsal, as well as in performance, and come to an understanding of the needs of the performers in both situations. Your role as a director of a jazz ensemble is one of an enabler and initiator rather than dictator. The better your group becomes the less they will need you.

It is a very generous and hands-off approach to conducting, promoting independence and self-reliance with the ultimate objective being that you are not required at all.

Count-ins and setting the groove

Counting in to the beginning of the piece or sections to be rehearsed is one of the most important things you will be doing as a director. This apparently simple task, if done incorrectly or unclearly, can lead to many problems and set you off on the wrong foot from the start.

The primary reason for jazz music traditionally having a count-in at the start rather than a downbeat from a baton is to do with the groove element of the music. There is no pulling around of the time feel, or ebb and flow of the pulse, as with classical music. In jazz there is nearly always an incessant pulse that all the members of the group have to lock into to be taking part effectively. Before the musicians start to play there is obviously no groove or pulse happening, so in order for everyone to lock into the same rhythmic feel straight away we need a count-in. So, the primary purpose of the count-in is two-fold – to bring everyone in together and to set the groove, feel and tempo before the music starts.

There are a few things you should consider before counting in. Think carefully about the tempo. The exact tempo you choose may be decided by various factors. For the most part these will be musical considerations such as style and mood. You will find that certain pieces really 'sit' at a particular tempo, and it will take a moment's thought to consider this.

There will also be technical considerations. Is there a particular ensemble passage that, if taken too fast, will be too difficult? Will the tempo be too slow for the breathing on certain phrases, or should you consider the stamina of the brass players if there are any long high notes? At which tempo does your rhythm section feel most comfortable?

Think carefully about the groove. What type of groove is it? It may be swing, Latin, rock or quite a free feel. Try to indicate something of the groove and feel in the count-in. Here are three examples representing by far the most common grooves in jazz:

1. Swing groove

The essence of swing is the emphasis on beats 2 and 4 of each bar allied to the quaver pushes providing syncopations around the main pulse. To indicate this groove in the count-in, click your fingers or clap your hands on beats 2 and 4. When you have everyone's attention and are sure everyone is focused on the pulse, say the count-in '1 – 2 –, 1 2 3 4'. You can also indicate some of the pushes characteristic to this style by placing the second '1' that you say on the 'and' of 4 in the first bar.

Example 1: Swing straight count-in

Swing

4/4	♩	𝄽	♩	𝄽		♩	♩	♩	♩
	×		×			×	×	×	×
	One,		two,			one,	two,	three,	four.

Example 2: Swing pushed count-in

Swing

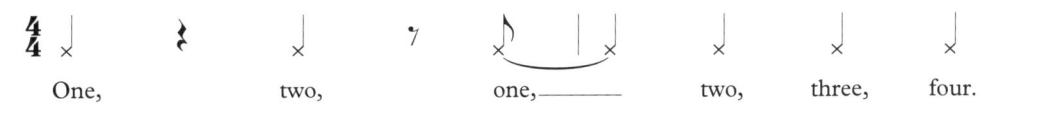

One, two, one,———— two, three, four.

2. Latin groove

Here you need to indicate the strong beats on 1 and 3 and the fact that there are straight quavers. Also bear in mind that there is a certain lilt to these quavers with a slight emphasis on every third quaver in a group of four. You can indicate this in your count-in by clicking or clapping on 1 and 3 while saying the count-in in the following way.

Example 3: Latin count-in

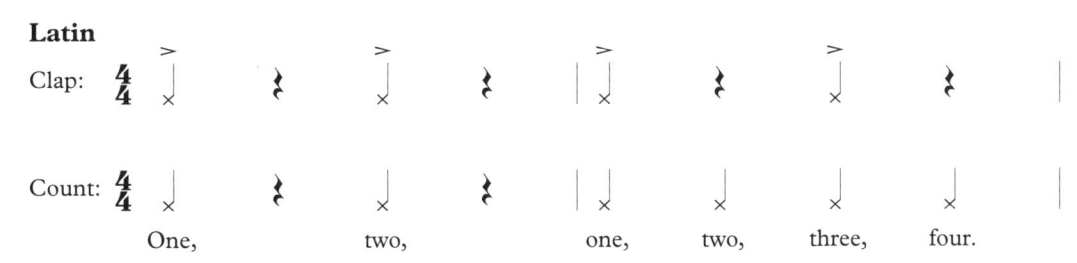

Latin

Clap:

Count:

One, two, one, two, three, four.

3. Rock

The important emphasis here is back on to beats 2 and 4 but with a 'straight-8' quaver pulse. Again, click or clap on 2 and 4. You can indicate the straight quavers by putting in 'ands' to your count-in.

Example 4: Rock count-in

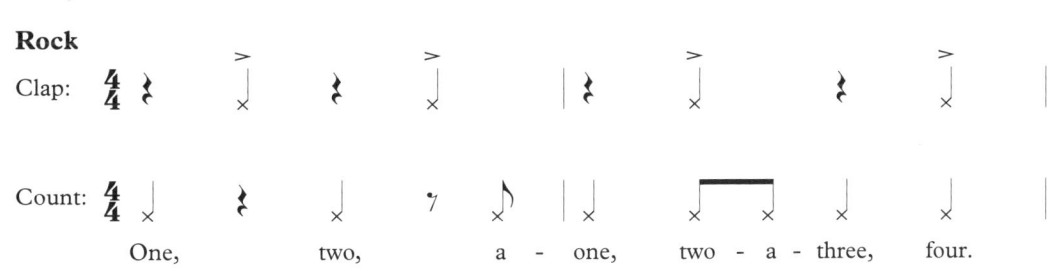

Rock

Clap:

Count:

One, two, a - one, two - a - three, four.

Tempos in rehearsal

You may need to rehearse things at different tempos in rehearsal. Difficult figures or ensemble sections may need slowing right down to get the fingers around them, or to follow fast reading passages. The problem here is that once a tempo has been established it will, to a certain extent, be fixed in the mind of the group.

A radical shift of gear can be very off-putting and so can be prepared in the following way. If a change of tempo is being used in rehearsal, make sure everyone has understood that the forthcoming count-in is going to be very different from what they have so far experienced. Click your finger or clap the new pulse for as long as you feel it takes to let the new tempo settle in. You can now count in the new tempo knowing that everyone has taken a few moments to hear and identify the new pulse.

There is now a much better chance of everyone locking in to the new tempo straight away, making the whole rehearsal more productive.

In conclusion

Do not underestimate the importance of a good count-in. It is not just a way of saying 'on your marks, get set, go' but is a means of communicating a lot of important musical information to the performers. Be thoughtful about the tempo and style of your count-in and always deliver it with positive authority.

How to cue sections

As discussed earlier, the compositions are all constructed in a modular way. There are many open repeats, with signs and codas together with optional interludes and backings. Logistically this could prove confusing unless very clear directions are given. Moving on to different sections of the piece will have to be rehearsed as much as any other aspect of the performance.

In the introduction we have already seen that the role of the director of a jazz ensemble is different to that of an orchestra or wind band conductor. Luckily you do not have to conduct every beat, as the rhythm section are taking care of the pulse and groove. This means that you are free to give a variety of signals more related to the structure of the piece. It will be useful as a director to build up a repertoire of stock signals that everyone understands.

The first signal you will need is one to show you are about to give a signal! This may sound strange but in the fray of a performance the musicians will have many distractions. They will either have their heads in the parts, will be in full flight of a solo, or be distracted by one thing or another. In order that everyone is aware that an important direction is coming up and that everyone in the group sees and understands it at the same time, their attention will have to be caught.

Try the sudden raising of a hand. This is very visual and, if done very positively and at the right moment, will guarantee to catch everyone's eye. Also remember to use this signal sparingly. Never call their bluff. Develop the habit in the players that whenever you do this they will need to look up for a crucial piece of information they cannot do without. You now have everybody's attention – let us look at the variety of signals you will need.

Cueing the next soloist

Ideally your soloists should have rehearsed the solo sections in such a way that they are aware of the form, and have a strong idea of how to break the solo up into choruses. However, the reality is that in the heat of the moment someone will lose their way and need a hand getting back into the form. A common problem is that if a soloist stops too early or too late then the next soloist starts playing straight away, across the form, and never gets back in. You can indicate the next soloist by pointing first and then giving a positive downbeat when they are to begin. Make sure that the current soloist knows they are to stop.

Always remember that the aim is to promote self reliance in the performers. Ideally they will have learnt to hear the form and choose how many choruses they wish to play. So, direct the solo section only if you think the help is required; as soon as there is a sign of growing self-reliance gradually withdraw the directions until the players are entirely independent and confident.

Cueing the backings to a solo section

Many of the solo sections will have accompanying backing figures that are entirely optional. If there are several solos during the performance it is probably better not to use the backings on every one. Also, to preserve an air of spontaneity, it is best to use them at will rather than in a predetermined fashion. You therefore require a signal to bring them in.

This has to be distinct from the other possible signals during the solo section, for instance indicating the next soloist or moving on to an ensemble section. Try tapping the back of your shoulders with your hand just before the backings are to come in then give a clear count-in. You can also mouth or shout the word 'backings'.

Indicating that a section is open

In many of the pieces there are what are called 'open sections'. These sections are vital to jazz composition in that they literally open up space, usually for some improvisation. It is crucial that you and your group get used to the concept of open sections, as it will give you the freedom to allow soloists their own space, and for you to construct the piece to suit the musicians involved. You must feel completely at liberty to create an open section wherever you feel it is appropriate, as well as opening up the sections indicated by the composer.

Open sections will take the form of a repeat section with an unlimited number of repeats. This will normally allow for a soloist to stretch out or to accommodate several soloists in the one section. To indicate that a section is open the director can make the following signal to the group. Hold up both hands and make two 'Os' with your thumb and index finger. The 'O' obviously signifies 'open', and you make two just to make it distinct from many one-hand signals you might use. Alternatively you can make a circular motion with one hand to indicate that this section is 'round and round' until cued.

An open section should always be repeated in its entirety. So in, for example, an eight-bar open section you might play 16, 24, 32 bars and so on, but never any number of bars that is not divisible by eight. Or, to put it another way, never cue another section in the middle of an open one.

Indicating the form

As a director you can serve a vital and useful role in pointing out the corners of the form during the solos. This should be done to provide reassurance that everyone is in the right place, rather than as a prop for everyone to rely on. If you feel this is needed then just give a strong downbeat at the appropriate moments, making sure that this signal cannot be confused with others such as moving on to the next section or cueing the next soloist.

Usually this signal is used in indicating the top of the form (e.g. the 33rd bar of a solo based on a sequence of 32 bars). However, sometimes you may need to point out other parts of the form like, for example, the B section. Where the form of the sequence is AABA over 32 bars, inexperienced players can get lost in the repeated A sections before the B section. If this happens, catch the lost player's eye and give a pre-determined signal for the B section. Obviously you will have to agree this in advance. A common signal is to mime playing chords on a piano, making an obvious movement across the imaginary keyboard to show that the harmony is changing (as it usually does for the B section).

Moving on to a new section

Now you have these long open sections which, as we have already said, are vital in breaking up the form and giving a flexible space to your performers. But how do you get out of them? You will have to give the same clear signal (that you are moving on to a new section) several times during one piece, and so must have a tried and tested method for this.

When you have made the decision to go on, first of all make sure that everyone has got time to see and respond to your direction. An ideal preparation for moving on is to indicate that the particular repeat you are in is for the last time. You need to communicate to the group that 'we're going on this time!', and you can do this by pointing forward with your whole arm. Be sure to indicate some sort of forward motion in this signal as this will help fix it in the players' minds that it means to 'go on'.

If done properly you will have given this signal in plenty of time, allowing you to give a count down of the last four bars. At the beginning of the last four bars hold up a hand showing four fingers, then three, then two and on the final bar indicate the last beats of the bar as a count-in. If this is something you only ever do to get from an open section into the following section, then it will become a failsafe method of direction you can rely on. Take time to practise it for your own benefit, before doing it with the group.

Using an interlude or a solo launch

Some pieces will have interludes and/or solo launches. These are designed as another way of breaking up the form and giving you and the performers the chance to shape the piece for yourselves. You can use them to allow the overall shape of the piece to 'breathe', or as a climactic build-up that will act as a launch to the next section.

Because of the fact that you can use these features where and when you like, we have occasionally written them at the end of the score and parts. This means that to use them the whole group will have to jump from where they are in the part to where the interlude is written. It is probably safest to have decided where the interlude will work, and use it in the same place or places each time to build up familiarity.

However, since this will most probably be in between solos or before moving on to a new section, you will have to devise a distinct signal to cue the interludes and launches. Try making the shape of the capital letter 'I' using two hands or the letter 'L' with one hand, then once this signal has been noticed by the whole group use the 'count-down' method as described in the last section.

Stopping a section

There may be times when you will need to stop elements of the performance. This might be a simple case of bringing the backing figures to a close so that the next soloist can come in. However, in more extreme circumstances it may be a matter of crisis management. There will inevitably be times where something goes wrong in performance, or when running something in rehearsal.

There are many different possibilities, but it is quite likely to be one of the following. A soloist may continue to solo when you have actually moved on to a new section. The front line may plough on to the ensemble chorus when you actually meant to cue the backings. Someone may have missed the fact that the section they are on is open, and may only have made the repeat twice and then gone on. There may be a direction on the part to play something 'second time only' which may have been missed. Either way what has happened is that some members of the band are playing when they should not and need to be told to stop.

Ideally you need a signal that is clear and decisive, but subtle enough that the audience does not cotton on to your impending disaster. Wading through the band and physically restraining the errant individual may be an effective means of damage limitation, but you run the risk of disrupting the 'cool' aspect of the performance!

Develop a signal that you use that means 'stop playing'. This will be your predetermined contingency plan to avert disaster. Try to make it directional, so that you can aim it at a certain player or area of the band, otherwise you will run the danger of bringing the entire performance to a halt when you only meant to stop one player.

Point to the players involved in the problem, and with the other hand make some sort of arresting gesture. If things get really desperate shout 'stop' and shake your head at the same time, though this is probably best used only in rehearsal.

Above all, try not to make the signal too recriminating, as you should try to bear in mind that you are teaching and expecting quite a high level of musical awareness. Again, if this signal is used only in certain circumstances, its meaning will be more clearly understood and consequently reacted to in the appropriate way.

In conclusion

Your repertoire of signals and directions will allow you to shape the compositions in rehearsal and in performance. They will combine to become your own personal signature as a director and, like any other aspect of technique, they can be improved upon with practice.

Do not be afraid to run sections in rehearsal solely with the aim of getting used to how the directions work. Navigating through the piece is as much a part of the performance as is playing the right notes. Also, remember that jazz music thrives on informality, so you should feel uninhibited in literally shouting directions at the group, even in performance. Do not be afraid to holler 'Open!', 'Going On!' or 'Last Time!', along with your signals and directions.

An energetic and entertaining display by the band leader can add significantly to the atmosphere of a concert, particularly if the audience are somewhat reserved or unsure of the appropriate means of response to the music.

Chapter 4: How to rehearse a solo section

These pieces are specifically designed as vehicles for improvisation. To improvise on the solo sections you will find certain information very useful. As discussed earlier in the chapter on improvisation, what we are doing is improvising with musical properties. The soloist is at liberty to improvise melodically, rhythmically and harmonically, letting your musical imagination create interesting lines, shapes and forms to play over these sequences. The musicians are improvising with the vocabulary of jazz, which includes styles and ideas borrowed and transformed by them from their own listening experience, be it from recordings or live gigs.

This section of the book aims to provide you and your group with a methodical approach to discovering how to deal with the improvised sections of the pieces. We will equip you with knowledge relating to melodic resources, rhythmic ideas and harmony, and will suggest ways of learning and experiencing these ideas as a group.

Preparation

There are a number of useful things you can do as a teacher in preparation for running a solo section rehearsal with your group.

Firstly, read the relevant chapter in this book for the piece you have chosen. Each piece in the series has its own dedicated chapter discussing important elements to do with performance, but most importantly on the solo sections. It will contain a detailed look at the harmony and related melodic resources as well as suggestions on vocabulary and ways to develop ideas.

Secondly, your knowledge of the score will be important. Take some time to familiarise yourself with the solo sequence from the score. Ideally you should learn to play through the harmonic sequence yourself at the piano. This does not have to be to any performing standard, so if you are not a pianist do not worry. It is mainly so that you, the teacher and band leader, have a thorough aural grasp of the harmonic movement of the form.

It is possible, for example, that your novice rhythm section could well play a wrong note just by missing one accidental. This could change the chord type radically from, say, major to minor or from major 7th to a dominant 7th. If you have a strong sense of what the sequence should sound like, you will be in a good position to correct and advise on the harmonic detail and form. It is vital that the rhythm section is giving out the right harmonic information to the band as a whole, as this is your starting point when exploring the harmony with the group.

Thirdly, look at the scale resources written on the part. One of the most important skills to acquire as a jazz musician is a knowledge of how to work out the melodic properties of a chord from the written chord symbol. This is often referred to as 'scale to chord theory'.

At the initial and intermediate level, whenever a chord symbol is written on the parts or in the score, we have also written out the scale properties of the chord. This is a convention we have adopted for educational reasons, and is not usual in most forms of chord notation you may see elsewhere. It will be useful for you to know exactly what information the performers are equipped with on the printed page so that you can talk to them about it, and refer them to certain details. For this reason the scale choices are given in the score as well as in the parts. Bear in mind, though, that they will have been transposed on the parts, so that where, in the score, you see a C^7 chord accompanied by the Mixolydian mode on C, the E♭ part has an A^7 chord with A Mixolydian as the scale resource.

In rehearsal

Set up the rhythm section

The first step is to rehearse the rhythm section, ensuring that they can play through the form of the sequence, following all the correct chord changes. Many pieces have sample bass lines and voicings for piano and guitar, which should help at this stage. It is important that the whole group, front line and rhythm section, hears and understands the context in which they are about to improvise.

Talk through the form

Once you are happy with the rhythm section you can start addressing the whole group. If they have been paying attention they will already have a strong idea of what is going on, as they have just heard you rehearse the rhythm section. To reinforce this new information try the following.

As the rhythm section play through the sequence, get everyone else to clap on important parts of the form. The sequence will probably break down into units of four or eight bars. Get the group to mark these sections out by clapping on the first beat of each of these units. You can also get them to shout out 'B section' or 'top' when they come to the appropriate sections. This will concentrate everyone's mind on listening intently to the rhythm section, trying to hear the sequence as a whole.

Sing the roots of the chords and important voice leadings (guide tones) along with the rhythm section. By doing this players will experience the key sounds in the sequence in real time and in a musical context. By singing roots and guide tones you are identifying and emphasising the nuts and bolts of the musical framework. More specific things to sing with the rhythm section will be outlined in the chapters on the individual pieces.

Teaching melodic properties

Now the group has a strong handle on the form, and has experienced the harmonic framework through singing and clapping, it is time to introduce some melodic ideas.

There are scales written out on the score and parts to help with the improvising. It is important to remember that these scales are there as a melodic resource, rather than as something to be played just because they fit the chords. It is not scale exercises we want to hear but melodic invention using the notes of the scale.

In order to have freedom and plenty of options available as an improviser it is necessary to achieve a certain level of dexterity with the relevant scale resource. This will require practice.

You can practise as a group first to give everybody an idea of what to do, but you can also suggest some things to practise individually. Let us take John Warren's piece, *Slice and Dice*, as an example. There is a solo section that uses just the Mixolydian mode, starting on G. Mixolydian is the 5th mode of the major scale, so here we are talking about the 5th mode of C major. This scale is also written out on the parts as a guide.

Example 5: Mixolydian, starting on G

Get the whole group to run up and down the scale to familiarise themselves with the pattern. Now get the group to play the arpeggio going up to the 7th and back down again, then perhaps up to the 9th. Ask them to play the scale in 3rds, using both ascending and descending patterns. Try also some rhythmic patterns using selected notes from the scale. All of these exercises can be set for private study as well as with the whole group and, if you would like more detailed exercises, there are many others in the chapters on the pieces later in this book. Refer to the chapter dedicated to the piece you have chosen and there you will find further scale resources and patterns that can be learnt and used in improvisations.

Finally, run some solos

You have now worked the rhythm section up to a good standard, taught the whole group how to hear the form and understand the basic framework of the sequence, and given everybody some melodic resources to play with. You can now run some solos.

Ask for volunteers or pick somebody who has done well with all the preparatory work. Try to involve as many members of the group as you can, and from the outset encourage even the most timid player to have a go. You never know who will eventually emerge as your star soloist.

Get the rhythm section to play one chorus before the soloists come in. Give everyone a short burst, allowing them enough time to acclimatise to the changes and feel their way.

Feedback session

Make sure every solo is met with encouragement and support from the whole group. It is of paramount importance that you create an environment where everyone feels they can contribute, and that their input is valued. Invite comments from the group to instigate a discussion on how they thought the solos went. You can ask what they liked about a particular solo, or what they thought of their own effort.

Encourage positive feedback, steering the comments towards specific, positive aspects of whatever is being discussed. Comments like, 'I really liked the way Dave held the long note right at the end of his solo and then did a fall off the end of it' or 'I thought Amy's solo was great because she just played two notes, but played them in loads of different ways...' are to be encouraged.

Always remember that the objective is to give encouragement whilst at the same time raising the general awareness of what works well. You are also enhancing everyone's ability to listen critically and intently, which is a skill that can be transferred into many other areas.

In conclusion

You have now gone through a rehearsal process that has covered the following aspects:

1. Preparation: making sure that you, the teacher or band leader, are completely on top of the material before you start.

2. Rhythm Section: coaching the rhythm section to a sufficiently high working standard.

3. Form: talking, singing and clapping through the basic framework of the sequence.

4. Melodic Resources: the group is given an approach to learning the scale resources and melodic properties to construct a solo.

5. Soloing: everyone in the group has tried an actual solo.

6. Feedback Session: everyone has had some sort of appraisal of how things went. Awareness was raised as to which were successful ideas, with a positive discussion of why they worked well.

Chapter 5: How to rehearse the ensemble section

This part of the book is concerned with rehearsing the written ensemble material and will also cover matters of style and interpretation. The main focus will be on the written material for the front line, but will include comments on how the rhythm section fits around, and sets up, the phrasing.

This section deals with how to interpret the written material, and how to perform it with the appropriate style, idiomatic inflection and nuance that the notation does not show. We will also look at rehearsal techniques and instrumental techniques, so as to familiarise you and your group with the conventions of jazz performance practice.

Phrasing

We have already seen that the interpretation of written jazz music requires stylistic understanding and listening experience. We have also seen that quaver subdivisions of the pulse can be numerous, and that subtle variations can affect the feel and groove quite radically. We can now look at phrasing and address the question of how to bring the music on the printed page to life by the use of accents, bends, dynamics and general stylistic nuances.

The concept of inner dynamics

Not all notes within a melodic line or phrase have equal importance. Some notes may be outlining crucial voice leadings in the harmony and some will be passing notes. Some notes may be part of a rhythmically important pattern, while some may just be ornaments of it. Anyone who has heard a 'quantised' computer-generated version of a melody will be able to tell you that any musical meaning is greatly diminished by the fact that all the notes are played equally in dynamic, placement and accent. A good musician will naturally phrase a melodic line in a way that informs the listener of the harmonic and rhythmic importance of each note. Look at the following phrase from *Slice and Dice* by John Warren.

Example 6: 'Slice and Dice' first rendition of the head

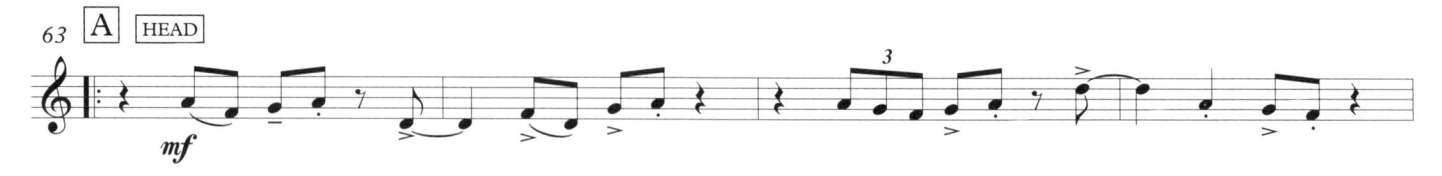

Observe the first four quavers of the head. Each of these four quavers should be played with a different emphasis. The first quaver is quite strong and positively placed as it is the first note we hear and is on the second beat of the bar.

The second quaver is an offbeat and an approach note to the G that follows it and should be played quite weakly. The third quaver is on a strong beat, and should have more emphasis but not as much as the first note. The last quaver in this four-note phrase is deliberately marked short, and is the note that makes the phrase syncopated and swinging. This should be given the most emphasis of the four.

So, we have four quavers in a hierarchy of importance according to their harmonic or rhythmic positions. To give these quavers their relative importance they must be played with varying dynamics. These dynamics on a local scale are what we call the 'inner dynamics' of the phrase.

This might seem an over-analytical and painstaking process to go through if you were to apply it to every single phrase. However, let us see how a few simple rules of inner dynamics can be applied to the whole head. Your group will soon be phrasing in a stylistic and groove-oriented way quite naturally once they grasp the concept.

We noticed that the last quaver in the pattern should be given more emphasis to bring out the syncopation. Throughout the whole head each phrase ends with a similar figure, so each can be treated in the same way. Similarly, all the other phrases have offbeat approach notes that can be hinted at, and some onbeat notes that deserve emphasis, but not as much as the syncopated ones. Basically, the same phrasing for the four-note pattern can be applied to the rest of the head.

Instrumental techniques for the front line

Now that the concept of inner dynamics is clear, and an understanding of swing quavers has been reached, we can talk about the repercussions of these stylistic devices for instrumental technique, which we can break down into three main areas, articulation, long notes and vibrato.

Articulation

Articulation in jazz is generally a lot clearer and more incisive than in many other areas of music. This is largely due to the strong rhythmic aspect of the music. As the front line are required to contribute rhythmically to the ensemble just as much as the rhythm section, they will have to articulate positively and with clarity.

Encourage the front line to tongue in a very forthright way, not only to bring out any accents, but also to commit to the rhythmic life of the music. As every brass and wind peripatetic teacher knows, one of the main problems for beginner instrumentalists lies in co-ordinating the articulation with the breath support. Another common problem is that of failing to support the sound with the air stream once the note has been articulated. This is why students are often encouraged to tongue the note gently, not explosively, and then provide a continuous steady support to the note. This is still good advice to hone basic instrumental technique. However, it should not discourage you from getting the students to play with a hard and pronounced attack when required. You will find that brass players will adopt this approach quite naturally and enthusiastically.

Reed players generally need more encouragement, as it is harder to achieve a clearly-tongued articulation, and the fear of making squeaks from over-blowing tends to dilute their conviction somewhat. Try to get reed players to avoid 'breathy' attacks or anything that sounds fuzzy, articulating strongly, with plenty of support from the diaphragm.

Long notes and vibrato

Jazz is associated with short clipped phrases and spiky syncopation. There are, of course, many long notes in the phrase structure as well. Long notes in classical music are usually played with an even and sustained sound, and these days the trend is away from vibrato. Long notes in jazz, however, tend to have swells in the dynamic, and make much use of vibrato. This helps add to the forward momentum and drive associated with this more rhythmic music.

The combination of the strong articulation, use of vibrato and dynamic swells does much to add musical interest and colour to the phrase and is an integral part of the style. A common technique is to hit the long note with a strong articulation, best described as a forte piano, stay on the low dynamic for most of the note, saving the crescendo until the end, then finishing with a tongue stop.

There are many forms of vibrato, all of which can be used through a wide spectrum of intensity. Ask your front line to experiment with vibrato using the lip or the air stream, or a combination of both. Trombonists can experiment with slide vibrato. Vibrato can be used in many different ways, but the most usual approach is to use vibrato that increases towards the end of the note. This means that intonation is not impaired, yet colour is added towards the end of the note.

Tongue stops

A tongue stop is a means of stopping the note to give a well-defined and rhythmic finish. The effect is achieved by placing the tongue in the way of the air stream at the end of the note, causing a clipped and abrupt end to a held note. This is really a way of placing an articulation on the end of the note, as opposed to letting it ring on or sound open-ended.

This technique not only tidies up ensemble playing but also contributes to the groove and general rhythmic drive. It is not necessary or desirable to use tongue stops all the time. They can be used selectively at appropriate moments in the music. If they are used in the wrong context or are overdone there is a danger that they can sound very harsh and ugly.

You can 'overcook' a tongue stop easily just by being too forceful. What is desired is a neat and well-defined close to the note, rather than an explosive noise that changes the pitch or quality of the note. Again, this technique slightly goes against the grain of orthodox instrumental technique.

A common problem with novice wind and brass players is the inability to stop a note in any other way than with the tongue. You must bear in mind that a significant part of their instrumental tuition may well be devoted to getting them to finish a note without the tongue to achieve a more open and resonant finish. They must be made aware that there are the two different techniques for differing musical contexts.

In conclusion, the group should be encouraged to articulate clearly and positively, use vibrato and tongue stops judiciously and add interest and colour to long notes by shaping them with dynamics.

Chapter 6: Jazz conventions/focus topics

It is often said that there is an art to every science and a science to every art. To understand some of the science behind the art of jazz improvisation, this chapter presents a series of theoretical topics that will be of direct relevance to learning to improvise on these eight pieces.

Swing quavers

In this series, all swing quavers are notated as ordinary, or straight, quavers. This is a recognised convention in written jazz music, and is considered easier to read than compound time, which itself is an inaccurate representation of what swing quavers actually do. Once the concept of swing quavers is understood, playing them becomes automatic.

The swing groove is the most common time feel in jazz music. It lends itself well to improvising as it has a strong pulse and an elasticity that invites syncopation and other rhythmically interesting patterns. Also, because the crotchet pulse is so strong, a very flexible approach to the quaver feel is an integral part of the style. It must be emphasised that this quaver subdivision of the beat in the swing groove is not an even metric division, with every quaver being equal (this is known as straight quaver subdivision, or just straight quavers, and is characteristic of classical music). Swing quavers are quite different in that they lean more towards a triple time feel, and have different stresses and accents according to where they are placed in the bar.

Swing quavers are an unequal division of the crotchet beat, and lie somewhere between quavers in compound time and straight (regular and even) quavers. A compound time concept of swing leads to too much emphasis of the onbeats (beats 1 and 3). Straight quavers are stiff and, if played to a swing groove, sound mechanical and stilted.

Here are some suggested exercises to help with the swing quaver feel. First of all you will have to get your rhythm section working, so we will look at drums, bass, piano and guitar in turn and see what they should be doing. Also refer to the sections in this book on the rhythm section for even more detail on this subject.

The drums lead the groove with a strong crotchet pulse on the ride cymbal. This crotchet pulse is often divided into quavers on beats 2 and 4, creating the typical basic ride pattern.

Example 7: Basic ride pattern

Swing

The hi-hat plays a crisp 2 and 4, while snare and bass drum contribute pushes on the 'and' of 2 and 4, and outline riff-like patterns.

Example 8: Two bars of swing feel drums

Swing

ride
floor hi-hat
snare
bass drum

The bass usually plays what is called a walking bass line, four crotchets in every bar which usually move in stepwise motion at a regular rhythmic pace, hence the name 'walking bass'. These crotchets should be placed very emphatically, making each one as long and resonant as possible.

The piano and guitar provide the harmonic content, and play riff-like interjections similar to that of the snare and bass drum combination of the kit. In a good rhythm section there will be much interplay between piano and drums, or guitar and drums. They will try to hook up to each other's rhythmic ideas, and mark out the form of the sequence together. They will also be responding to the soloist by filling space and responding to any rhythmic or thematic ideas.

To sum up, there is basically a strong crotchet pulse with the emphasis on beats 2 and 4, around which syncopated quaver interjections are placed.

Once you have achieved the desired sound and feel from your rhythm section, and explained the role of each rhythm-section instrument to the group, try the following exercise. Get the rhythm section to play at a medium tempo of about crotchet = 120. They should mark out four-bar or eight-bar phrases, and you can agree to mark out a chosen tonal centre. Try just playing on G. Once this has settled ask the front line to play this pattern.

Example 9: Front line pattern

The front line should be swinging the quavers quite naturally without being told to, but to raise awareness and to get everybody thinking about the feel, try the following.
 • Instruct the front line to play completely straight quavers, and point out how different this sounds and feels.
 • Now switch to compound time feel (i.e. 12/8). Observe the difference.
 • Go back to straight quavers, but this time accent the offbeat quaver.
 • Try compound time again, but with the last triplet quaver accented.

• Try straight quavers again and on your direction let the group relax the feel, just a little, towards the compound time feel.

• The group should now be acutely aware of how their interpretation of the quaver division effects the entire feel and groove of the ensemble. They should now also realise the flexibility of the feel and therefore be more conscious of the way they phrase.

To develop the exercise you can try faster or slower tempos. You will find that the faster the tempo the more appropriate it will seem to use a 'straighter' (more equal) subdivision. Conversely, the slower the tempo the more suitable a triple time feel will become. Remember that if either a purely straight or triple time subdivision is used with no offbeat accents, the feel will become stilted and mechanical, whatever the tempo. The most important thing to remember though is that we are dealing with an aural tradition here, so the group will never swing unless you actually hear a good swinging rhythm section, either live or from recordings.

There are many other rhythmic patterns that you can use. The following examples will give variety to the exercise and provide rhythmic vocabulary. Run them in the same sequence as the first example.

Example 10: Rhythmic vocabulary on swing quavers

Functional tonality vs. non-functional tonality

You do not have to be a music theory boffin to use this book, but it will help if you have a basic understanding of tonality and how it works. We refer to two kinds of tonality throughout this book, functional and non-functional. The first behaves like classical harmony in the sense that a chord of II followed by a chord of V^7 both prepares, and therefore defines, the chord (and 'home' tonality) of I.

The second is still tonal in the sense that there are recognised configurations of notes (triads, dominant 7ths and so on) but they behave more like the non-functional tonality to be found in music at the end of the nineteenth century. In this sense you might have a series of dominant 7ths that, whilst being related in a tonal sense, do not 'define' the chord five steps below as their 'home' chords. Do not worry if you find this a little confusing at this stage, just try to be flexible in your acceptance of how the various chords that make up the language of jazz can work together.

Scale to chord theory

First, a word about enharmonic re-spellings. Chord symbols are primarily a means of notating the essential harmonic information to the performer in the most practical way possible. We must remember that the performer has to respond to this notation in real time, that is, as the music is actually happening. Consequently we find that chord symbols occasionally use enharmonic spellings that are not entirely correct in the strictest academic sense, but are chosen for their practicality and ease of use. An interesting parallel can be drawn between modern chord symbol notation and figured bass notation. Both contain enough information for the performer to voice the chord correctly at sight, but both rely on the performer's experience to interpret the function and context of the harmony. This might manifest itself as, for example, the third of a chord of E^7 sometimes being spelled as A♭ if the voice leading dictates (e.g. if the surrounding notes are all flats).

Every harmonic configuration contains within it certain latent melodic properties. Put more simply, every chord suggests a collection of notes (i.e. a scale) from which melodies can be crafted. In order to create melody, the improvising musician needs to understand the melodic properties of the harmony he or she is playing over. As harmony in jazz is notated in the form of chord symbols, the jazz musician needs to know the melodic properties associated with these chord symbols, in other words, the scale to chord theory.

For the initial level of this series there are certain basic chord types that are used in the composition of the pieces. There is a chord chart on page 77 which acts as a complete reference for basic voicings and the relevant scale resources, but here we will show a few examples of how the scale is derived from the chord. This first chord symbol of Cmaj^7 denotes that above the root note of C is a major 3rd (E♮), and the major 7th (B♮).

Example 11: C major⁷ chord and scale

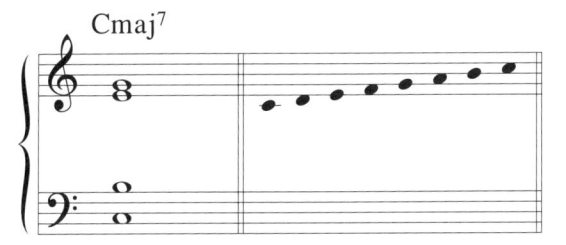

[Musical notation: Cmaj⁷ chord and C major scale]

In all chord symbols some information is taken for granted. In this case there is no reference to what type of 5th is being used, so we assume that there is a perfect 5th. Likewise there are no references to any chromatic alterations to any of the other notes (such as ♯11, for example) so we will assume they are all unaltered, or natural. Therefore if we add all the passing notes between the arpeggio notes of this chord we complete the major scale from the root note, in this case the C major scale.

Note the important inclusion of the B♮ (the major 7th) in the voicing. This note is here to colour the chord rather than act as a leading note pulling towards C. You now know that all major 7th chords have the major scale as their melodic resource. This is a collection of notes you should be familiar with in every key, so now there is no 'maj⁷' chord that you cannot improvise over.

Now consider this chord:

Example 12: C⁷ chord and scale

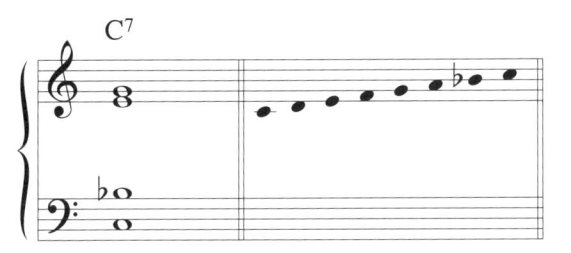

[Musical notation: C⁷ chord and scale]

This is the chord symbol for a dominant 7th. It is chord type V in the classical 'roman numeral' system of describing harmony. This is basically a root note above which are added a major 3rd, a perfect 5th and a flattened 7th. It is one of the most common chord types used in jazz, and therefore has one of the simplest shorthand names of just C⁷. So, whenever you see a '7' on its own after a chord name, you should remember that it is simply a major arpeggio with a flattened 7th or, put in classical terms, a dominant 7th. Because the flattened 7th is so common in jazz, convention dictates that it is usually referred to simply as 'the 7th'. This is not to be confused with the major 7th of the major scale, which would be referred to as a 'major 7th' or 'maj⁷'.

A word of warning – do not think that, just because it is a dominant 7th in shape, it can only happen on the dominant (i.e. chord V) of the key. The 7th chord as we see it here is probably the most common chord in jazz. Composers use it in any number of ways, and not always as a dominant. You may notice that we previously described the 7th chord as chord 'type' V. This is deliberately to distinguish it from being a dominant in a functionally tonal sense.

The scale resource for the 7th chord is the Mixolydian mode, which is simply a major scale with a flattened 7th. Put another way, it is the 5th mode of the major scale. In this instance it is the 5th mode of F major. As we have already seen, just because it is the 5th mode of F major does not mean the piece is in F, it is simply a way of describing the collection of notes. Once you have grasped the concept of the 7th chord, and how it can be used in any number of places without implying a strictly functional dominant relationship, you are well on the way to understanding one of the basic principles of jazz harmony.

Now let us look at the minor 7th chord and its scale relationship.

Example 13: Cm^7 chord and scale

This is Cm^7. The chord symbol 'm^7' denotes the minor triad with a 7th included. Here, as we have already seen, convention dictates that the 7th is the flattened 7th, in this case a B♭. For all minor chords you should assume that the 7th is always the flattened 7th unless otherwise stated. There are many different minor scales used in jazz, the most common one being the Dorian, which is the 2nd mode of the major scale. It fits well over this basic minor chord voicing.

Sometimes composers add other notes from the scale to the basic chord. It is important to realise that if the number written next to the chord symbol is a 9, 11 or 13 it does not necessarily change the function of the chord, nor the scale resource. For example C^9 is still a dominant using Mixolydian mode, there is just a 9th in the voicing as well. Similarly Cmaj^9 is still a major chord using the ordinary major scale (with a major 7th as indicated in the chord name) and just has a 9th in the voicing of the chord. Now let us look at the final example: C^{7}sus^4.

Example 14: C^{7}sus^4 chord and scale

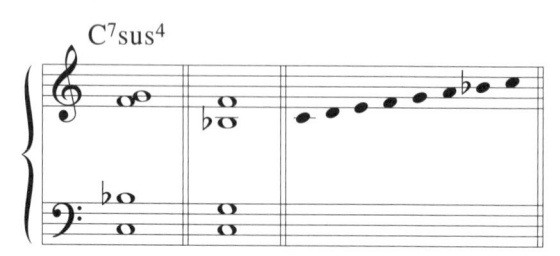

As by now you may have come to expect, this is still a dominant 7th, except that here the 4th, in this case an F♮, is in the voicing rather than the 3rd. As a lot of jazz harmony involves colourations of chords, this 4th, although technically 'suspended' in the sense of a 4–3 or 9–8 classical suspension, does not have to resolve.

Because it has no 3rd in the voicing this chord type is much more open than the fixed 7th chord. As there are no chromatic alterations to the chord the scale resource is still Mixolydian, just as for an ordinary dominant. However, the soloist would probably avoid playing the 3rd except as a passing note.

Guide tones

Guide tones are a means of plotting a linear route through a chord sequence, and they are very useful in bringing out important movements in the chord changes. If the soloist manages to target the guide tones in his solo, he or she can be sure of outlining the harmonic movement in the sequence.

As we have seen from the previous section, the notes in a chord which define the chord type and its function are most commonly the 3rds and 7ths. Consequently, the best notes to use as guide tones through a sequence are the 3rds and 7ths. Play through the following examples at the piano with the guide tones in the right hand and the root note in the left. This gives you the bare bones of the harmonic sequence, but enough to hear all the essential movement. A soloist pinpointing this guide tone route in an improvised melody would therefore be outlining the chord sequence at the most basic level. For more information on guide tones, refer to the focus topics chapter of the intermediate level Teacher's Book.

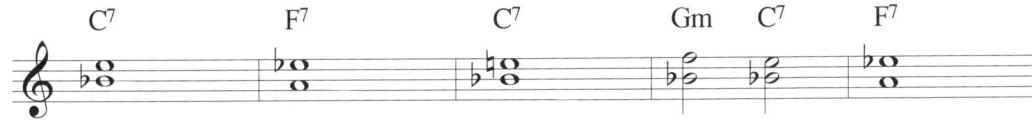

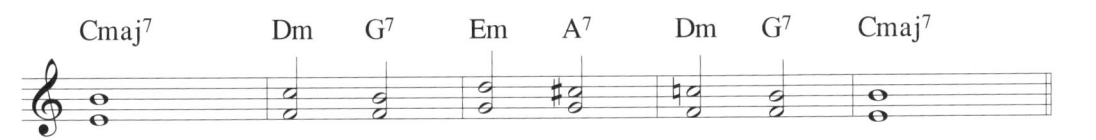

Example 15: Guide tones

The II–V–I cadence

The II–V–I cadence is one of the main building blocks in jazz harmony. It is a means by which tonal centres, both local and long-term, are prepared, arrived at and reinforced. It is important for an improviser to recognise that Dm⁷ followed by G⁷ is preparing the way for the 'home' tonal centre of C major. Unlike the 'floating' dominant 7th we described earlier, this cadence plays a clearly functional role in defining a key centre.

The use of recognisable diatonic harmony in a non-functional, but nevertheless tonal, manner is analogous to the approach found in some of the works of Debussy, Stravinsky and Satie.

We can see from the music example below that if you arpeggiate each of the notes in the major scale, different chord types are generated.

Example 16: Chords from the major scale

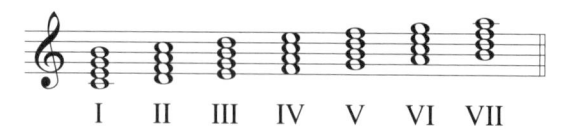

I II III IV V VI VII

From this we can extract chord II, chord V and chord I to create a cadence.

Example 17: The II-V-I cadence

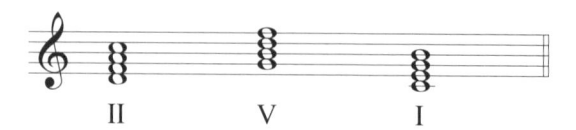

II V I

We can of course write out this progression with better voice leading and spacing. The G chord here is voiced as a G^9 but, as we have already seen, this does not affect its melodic properties.

Example 18: The II-V-I voiced

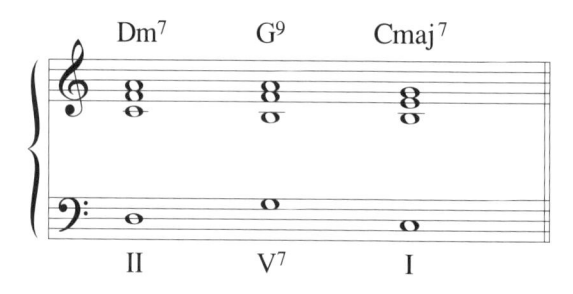

Dm^7 G^9 $Cmaj^7$

II V^7 I

Chord II is a minor 7th chord, chord V is a dominant and chord I is a major 7th chord creating in this instance a progression of Dm^7, G^7, $Cmaj^7$. As each of these chords is generated from the same scale, the melodic resources for all three chords are derived from the same scale as well. In this case it is the C major scale. It is important to know that one scale can be played over all three chords in a II–V–I.

A more satisfying approach, however, would be to pick out some of the linear movement in this sequence. The following examples use C major as the melodic resource but also describe the harmonic movement by outlining the guide tones.

Example 19: The II-V-I with guide tones

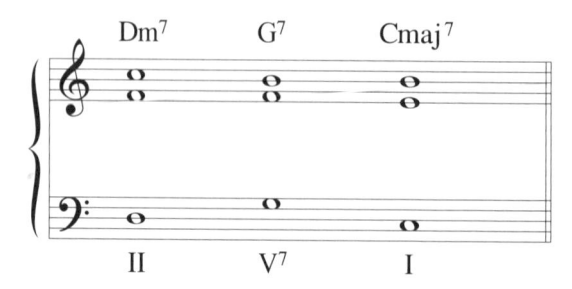

Dm^7 G^7 $Cmaj^7$

II V^7 I

Example 20: Melody using guide tones

Dm^7 G^7 $Cmaj^7$

The basic twelve-bar blues sequence

The twelve-bar blues is probably the most important form for jazz improvisation. All of the major figures in jazz music have spent a lot of time addressing the blues and have found it, by the very nature of its simplicity, to be a constant challenge and inspiration. Firstly, let us look at the basic concept of the harmonic relationships in a blues sequence. Remember that all the chord types are dominant 7th chords.

Example 21: Blues chord progression in C with guide tones

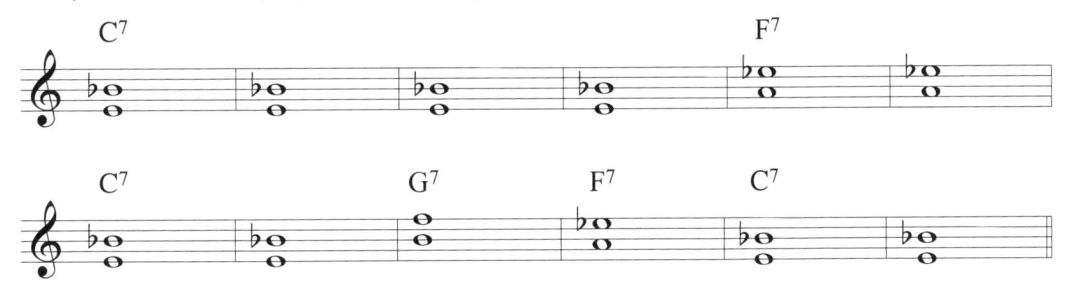

As we saw at the beginning of this chapter, this does not mean that all the chords actually function as dominants in the strictest sense of purely functional tonality.

Chord I is in fact C⁷ in this instance. This is the home key. The flattened 7th of B♭ is really a colouration of the C chord rather than a functionally dominant 7th.

So, C⁷ in this context is not the dominant of a tonal centre in F. We are clearly 'in' the key of C, even though the home chord has a flattened 7th for added colour.

Bearing this in mind, do not be confused by what happens next, which is a movement to F⁷. It is important to realise that this is not a V–I movement from C⁷ to F, but a movement from the home key of C (as articulated by the use of chord I) to the subdominant, F (chord IV). Again the F chord is coloured by a flattened 7th (E♭).

After a short period of time on the subdominant we return to the home key of C, again to the chord type of a (non-functioning) dominant, that is, C⁷. We are now two thirds of the way through the sequence. Traditionally, the last third of the sequence starts with the true dominant, which in this case is G⁷. This returns to the home key not via a perfect cadence, such as IV–V–I, but through the progression of 7th chords V–IV.

So we see that the blues sequence does rely on a sense of movement between the tonic, subdominant and dominant relationships inherent to the concept of tonality, but does so in a slightly unorthodox way. This is a vital concept to grasp in understanding the whole of jazz harmony.

In jazz harmony it is the root movement and the voice leading which make the most tonal sense, but without every chord type necessarily functioning in a traditional way. There are many parallels to be drawn between this harmony and that of Debussy and his contemporaries.

It should be seen as no accident that the full development of a harmonic language for jazz came at the time that Debussy's music was achieving common currency.

You can also view this concept of harmony as a result of a non-western assimilation of the laws of tonality. We must remember that tonality is a system that took hundreds of years to develop and is by no means a definitive approach to organising music. If the most important elements to a type of music are rhythm, improvisation and melodic line, as is indeed the case for many cultures outside Western classical tradition, then it is quite likely that, when confronted suddenly with tonality, these cultures would have adapted and modified the harmonic language accordingly.

As far as soloing over a blues sequence is concerned, any number of approaches can be taken. At the most basic level there is the resource of the blues scale, and this can be used throughout the entire sequence. However, although this approach provides a lot of scope for stylistic inflection and idiomatic language, it does not actually outline the harmonic progression.

Example 22: Blues scale in C

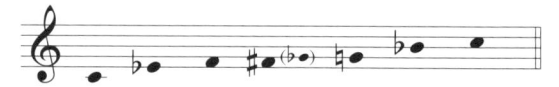

As well as playing interesting lines, the improviser should aim to add more musical meaning to his or her solo by outlining the form. This is primarily done by observing the harmonic movement.

As discussed earlier in this chapter, the harmonic movement can be outlined by using the guide tones based on the 3rds and 7ths of the chords, and the appropriate scale resources. This approach, combined with use of the blues scale, will create a solo that both describes the chord changes and remains true to the blues idiom. More on twelve-bar blues can be found in the focus topics chapter of the intermediate level Teacher's Book.

Licks

The word 'licks' is a common term among jazz and rock musicians. Put simply, licks are prepared melodic phrases. They are melodic fragments that the musician has learned, becoming part of his or her vocabulary. These licks may be ideas borrowed from records, or from other performers in a live situation, or they may be of the player's own invention. Whatever their origin they constitute an integral part of the musician's vocabulary and style.

Just as a player gets confidence from knowing a scale resource for a particular chord, so he or she is encouraged by having melodic resources on which to fall back if the well of creativity runs dry. This is not to encourage endless regurgitation of well-drilled licks, but rather to create confidence in players who may need a little help.

It can be argued that the use of licks can detract from the truly improvised approach as a lick is something that has been prepared earlier, and is therefore not spontaneous improvisation. However, if we use the parallel with language, we can see that you can say something spontaneous while still using known vocabulary and familiar turns of phrase.

Licks are a great way for an inexperienced player to build up his or her vocabulary. The novice improviser will be greatly encouraged by finding some licks that have strong references to the melodic language of jazz. They can then use these building blocks and points of departure for developing their own ideas.

It is important for developing players to learn to use licks creatively. For example, if a player decides to use a lick from someone else's solo that is fine. But encourage them to play the lick in all keys, thereby increasing their dexterity. Also, have them play the lick, then create an answering phrase using an aspect of the original lick, such as rhythmic repetition, or the shape of the melodic cell transposed to a different level. Here are two examples of licks, each of which is followed by an answering phrase that somehow mirrors the original lick. Notice how the lick is subtly altered to follow the chord progression.

Example 23a: Lick with answering phrase

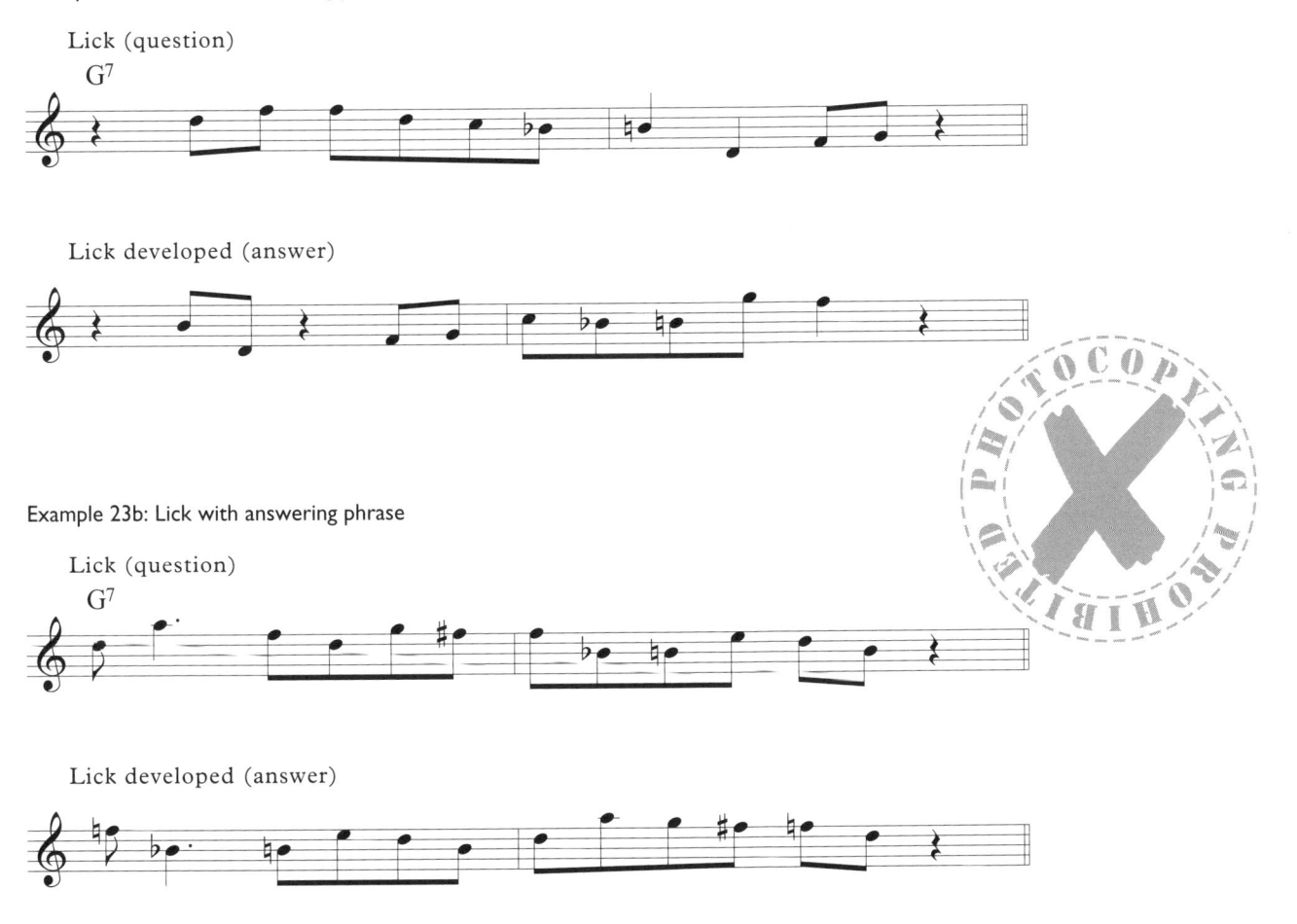

Lick (question)

Lick developed (answer)

Example 23b: Lick with answering phrase

Lick (question)

Lick developed (answer)

Not only will this encourage the players to think creatively about how to use licks, but it will also significantly enhance their ability to develop a solo with a sense of coherence and structure.

Each of the chapters dedicated to the solo sections of the pieces provides vocabulary and basic melodic ideas in the form of written out examples. In addition to this, many of the pieces deliberately use melodic material that can be lifted by the soloist and used in his or her improvisations. For instance *Straw Boss* uses several riffs for the backing figures to the solo sections, while the head in *Slice and Dice* is a series of short melodic fragments, all of which could be used as starting vocabulary.

Also, the accompanying CD at the back of the book will provide examples of how other jazz musicians have dealt with the material. In the true spirit of jazz you are, of course, at liberty to borrow their ideas as well.

Turnarounds

We have seen how a tonal area can be defined by the use of a II–V–I, so, for example, the key of C is reinforced by a progression through Dm and G^7. This principle can be extended to create the device commonly known as a 'turnaround'.

In a turnaround the home key is stated, moved away from, and returned to by way of a cadential progression. Here is the most common turnaround. In this example we have voiced out the chords, indicating the root movement and the guide tones.

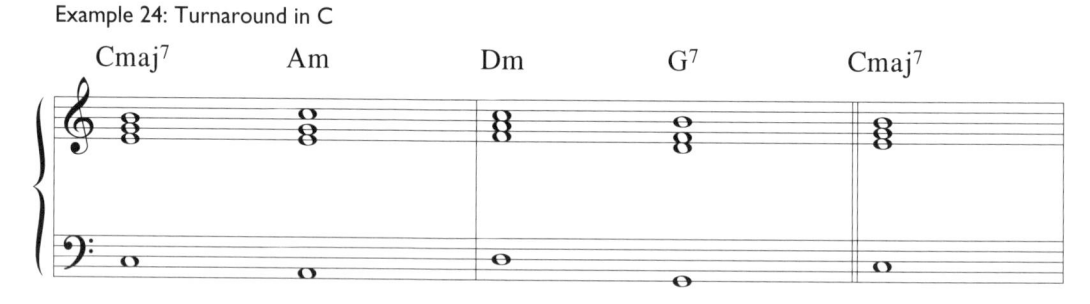

Example 24: Turnaround in C

This will probably be a familiar sound, as it is used commonly as a 'vamp' or 'repeat till ready' filler in all sorts of music. There are many variations on this form, using extensions, tritone substitutions and chromatic approach chords, but they all perform the same function, namely to reinforce the home key.

Part Two - The Pieces

Art's Groove
Composer: Frank Griffith

Solos

The main solo section is very flexible in that it can be treated very simply as well as offering scope for development for the more advanced student. It is a typical 32-bar sequence in AABA form.

The A sections

First, let us look at an approach that uses the blues scale. This scale, starting on F, will work very well on the A sections of the form, giving plenty of scope for melodic colour and stylistic inflection. Here is the blues scale on F, followed by some basic vocabulary using the scale.

Example 1: Blues scale on F

Example 2: Basic vocabulary

You can teach the group various fragments of the blues scale by leading a call–and–response session. Play them some phrases, then encourage them to pick out your ideas by ear. Do not feel the need to explain what is happening in the notes and rhythms until they have grasped the phrase. It is nearly always better to use your ears first, and then either to work out or be told what you are playing.

Here are some simple phrases to get you going. Notice they are all small rhythmic ideas using certain notes in the blues scale. Play or sing a phrase to the players and then, after a one-bar rest, ask them to play the motif back to you. Repeat each idea round and round until some fluency is achieved, then mix up the ideas. Get members of the group to make up a fragment for everyone to learn in the same way, or prepare some more of your own. This should be an enjoyable way of developing the vocabulary and aural ability of your group.

Example 3: Call and response

The B section

The B section is based on the II–V–I cadence to C major, with the last two bars being a II–V in F to take us back to the tonal centre of the A section. Here is the chord sequence of the B section written out with the guide tones.

Example 4: Bridge guide tones

As we have already seen, the guide tones are based on the 3rds and 7ths of the chords, and plot an aural map through the sequence to bring out the parallel movement. Soloing by using the guide tone movement is always a reliable option, as your melodic line will inevitably describe the harmony well.

If you have read the section on the II–V–I cadence you will know that it is possible to use the same scale over all three chords that make up this progression. Therefore the scale resource for the B section can be C major for the first six bars, followed by F major for the last two. Here is an example of how a melodic line can be created using these simple scale resources and the guide tones.

Example 5: Melodic line using scale resources and guide tones

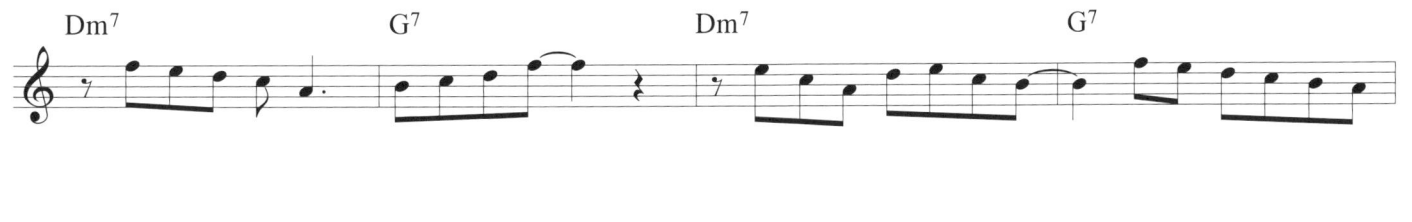

For rehearsal purposes you could get the rhythm section to loop the B section and allow everybody some time to experiment with the relevant II-Vs. Alternatively you could work on the II-Vs separately, only putting the whole B section together when everyone is comfortable with the progression.

Developed ideas for the A section

The blues scale allows for a strong stylistic approach and allows you to be very improvisatory. However, there comes a point where the sound of it can become rather tired, with both performer and listener wanting to hear some more harmonic detail in the melodic line. Using different scale choices and targeting key harmonic notes can sound refreshing and revitalising.

In the following paragraphs you will find a suggested approach for widening the scale resources available to your soloists. The theory of what is suggested may appear quite complex, especially for a piece pitched at relative beginners, and we certainly do not advocate that you attempt to teach it to your band. However, it would be useful for you as the teacher to know some of the theory, and to have a more extensive repertoire of choices to share with your students as they develop.

Always bear in mind that, although throughout this book we give you basic resources in the form of scales and motifs, these are by no means the only choices available. Part of the enjoyment of jazz is discovering for yourself what works for you, and what does not.

So, bearing that in mind, here are some ideas to help you develop the soloing on this sequence.

Try using scales derived from B♭ melodic minor. By using this scale on the A section you are accessing some interesting chromatic extensions.

B♭ melodic minor starting on F generates the 5th mode, known as 'Mixolydian ♭13', which turns the F7 into F7(♭13).

B♭ melodic minor starting on E♭ generates the 4th mode, known as 'Lydian dominant', which turns the E♭7 into E♭7(♯11).

This adds a new flavour to the improvised lines, and adds variety by getting away from the blues sound.

Example 6: Scales derived from B♭ melodic minor

You can also try using just the Mixolydian mode on F7 and then the Lydian dominant on E♭7. Let us compare these two scales.

Example 7: Mixolydian on F⁷

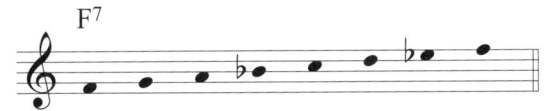

Example 8: Lydian dominant on E♭⁷

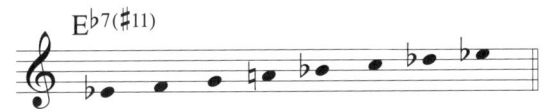

You will have to make appropriate shifts from the use of a D♮ to a D♭.

At the end of each A section notice that there is a harmonic shift up a semitone, from F⁷ to G♭⁷. This is useful in marking out the form, as it punctuates the end of each A section. Scale choices abound for this chord. You can think of it as Mixolydian derived from B major, or as Lydian dominant derived from the 4th mode of D♭ melodic minor. Fortunately, if this is too much science and algebra for you, the F blues scale will get you by fairly convincingly over this section.

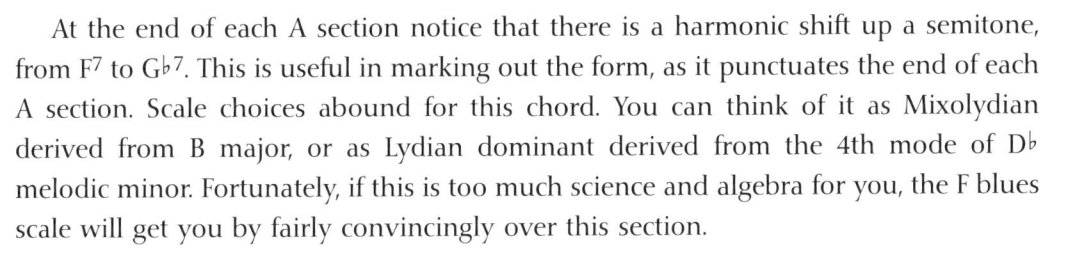

To develop the B section

Scale resources are suggested on the score and parts, and these offer very good starting points for the soloists. The more adventurous improviser may like to try using some chromatic passing notes within the scale resources suggested. To raise awareness of how this can be done, try giving the players a simple motif based on chord tones (i.e. any note from the given chord) and the given scale choices. Make it simple, consisting of only a handful of notes. Then ask the players to decorate their phrases by adding chromatic passing notes.

Here is an example of the phrase with chromatic decorations.

Example 9: Phrase with chromatic decorations

Azul

Composer: Mike Sheppard

Solos

This solo section is constructed mainly from two chord types, a 'sus⁴' chord and a minor 9th chord. This lends itself well to plenty of open blowing, using just a couple of scale resources for the whole section. The optional backing figures can lead the soloist through the form, marking out all the important corners. This is an ideal chord sequence for a beginner in many respects, with the pacing of the AABA structure providing plenty of space to feel your way and get comfortable with some basic chord types.

The A sections

All the A sections stay on a B♭7sus chord throughout. Here is this chord.

Example 1: B♭7sus chord

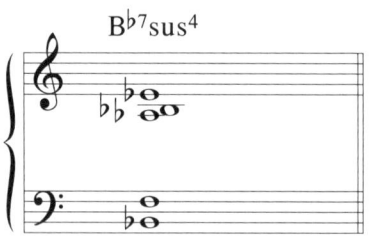

It is important to realise that 'sus⁴' chords differ from dominant chord types only in that they omit the 3rd from the voicing, replacing it with a 'suspended' 4th. As you know from reading the chapter on jazz conventions earlier in this book, very often in jazz harmony notes are added to a chord for colour rather than for a functional harmonic use.

The 'sus⁴' chord in this context is a good example, as the 4th here is not really suspended in the classical sense, where we would expect it to resolve downwards. In fact it never resolves. It is probably better to think of the chord as having an added 4th rather than a suspended 4th. Having said that, because of our ears being inevitably tuned to tonality, we cannot help but hear this chord not as a consonance, but rather as a restless sound wanting to lead somewhere. This is why these chord types are such fun to blow on, because they at once have an open and resonant sound while still seeming to have an air of expectancy. For further investigation into the 'sus⁴' chord, listen to *Maiden Voyage* by Herbie Hancock and *Yes or No* by Wayne Shorter.

As far as the voicing of a sus chord is concerned, it is useful to think of a major triad built on the flattened 7th. In this case it would be an A♭ major triad with a B♭ in the bass.

Example 2: A♭ major triad, with B♭ in bass

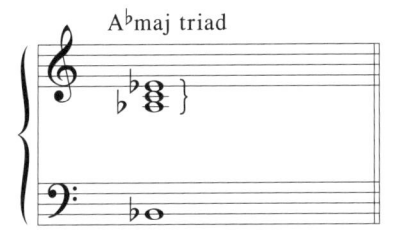

[Musical notation: A♭maj triad]

Being essentially a dominant chord type, the scale resource is still just the Mixolydian mode. However, being a sus chord with the 3rd omitted from the voicing, it will destroy the feeling of the sus chord if the major 3rd is played too prominently. It is for this reason that the suggested scale resource printed in the parts actually omits the 3rd completely, and is in fact an A♭ pentatonic starting on B♭.

This is to avoid the likelihood of the 3rd being played in the wrong context. The 3rd should be used with care and in fact should really only be used as a passing note, if at all. Here is some starting vocabulary to play on the B♭7 sus chord. Note the use of the A♭ triad to target the 7th, 9th and 11th (which is the same as the 4th), and how its major 3rd (C) is used in the suggested melodic fragment.

Example 3: Vocabulary on B♭sus

[Musical notation]

The B section

After 16 bars on the B♭7 sus chord, the B section takes us to a new tonal centre. This is Cm$^{9(\flat 6)}$. In the jazz conventions chapter we talked about the importance of scale to chord theory. The most common minor scale to use in jazz is the Dorian mode, which is the 2nd mode of the major scale. This mode is characterised by having a major 6th, which in this case would be an A♮. However, seeing as an A♭ has been particularly prominent in the preceding chord, it makes better aural sense for the A♭ to be preserved in the Cm⁹ chord as well. This means that the scale resource is not Dorian but Aeolian, the 6th mode of the major scale which contains a flat 6th.

Example 4: C Aeolian scale

Thus the scale resource for both the B♭sus chord and the Cm⁹⁽♭⁶⁾ chord are generated from the same 'parent scale'. B♭sus uses the 5th (Mixolydian) mode of E♭ major and Cm⁹⁽♭⁶⁾ uses the 6th (Aeolian) mode of E♭ major. Here is an example of some vocabulary to use for the B section.

Example 5: Vocabulary for the middle eight

In the jazz conventions chapter we saw how important it is to outline harmonic movement in your improvised melodic line. This is done by targeting both the guide tones and the important differences in the scale resources. As there are no differences in the parent scales for both chords, merely using the correct scale will not suffice in describing the harmonic movement between the two chord types. Certain degrees of the scale will have to be emphasised according to which chord you are on. It is the context in which the D♮ is played that is the key here.

As we have already seen, the D in the 'sus⁴' chord should be omitted, or used as a passing note, as it is the major 3rd and will destroy the suspended 4th if used without care. However, the D♮ in the minor 9th chord is in fact the 9th and is a very important part of describing this sound.

So, this is the solution to soloing on this piece. On the A sections use Mixolydian mode starting on B♭, taking care of the context of the 3rd if you use it at all. On the B sections, use Aeolian mode starting on C making sure you target a D♮ to target the 9th and to distinguish it clearly from the previous sus chord.

Lastly, observe that there is a dominant root movement at the end of the B section but the move to the dominant is made easier to solo over by the use of F⁷sus to Fm⁷, thereby obviating the need for a different scale resource for this important musical corner.

52 Azul

Bear Cave Blues

Composer: Malcolm Miles

Solos

This is an elongated version of the standard twelve-bar blues, this time in G. It is actually a 24-bar blues, being just a simple rhythmic augmentation of the basic twelve-bar format. This does not make it more difficult to solo on, but rather makes it easier, in that it gives the soloist double the time to think about the chord changes and scale options. As with most of the soloing in this series, there are simple ideas to get the ball rolling, with plenty of scope for development.

As detailed in the chapter on jazz conventions, the harmonic essence of the blues consists of dominant 7th chord shapes built on the roots of I, IV and V. Despite all of the chords being dominant shapes, it is very apparent to the listener that the sequence is a journey from tonic to subdominant, going back to the tonic, followed by a move to the true dominant which returns to the tonic again.

Let us look at the pacing of this format in the ordinary twelve-bar version.

G^7/// | //// | //// | //// |

C^7/// | //// | G^7/// | //// |

D^7/// | C^7/// | G^7/// | //// ||

Note that this is slightly different from, and in fact simpler than, the example given in the jazz conventions chapter. What they both have in common, however, is how the twelve bars are divided up. The twelve bars can be broken down further into three groups of four bars. See how each of the four-bar divisions starts with a different chord. The first four bars are the tonic, the second four the subdominant, and the third and final four-bar group starts with the dominant. Although this sequence varies from the example given in Chapter 6, they both share the same pacing of the root movements. This is common to all basic blues sequences.

Here is the actual 24-bar sequence from *Bear Cave Blues* written out. It is an exact rhythmic augmentation of the one above.

Example 1: 24-bar sequence

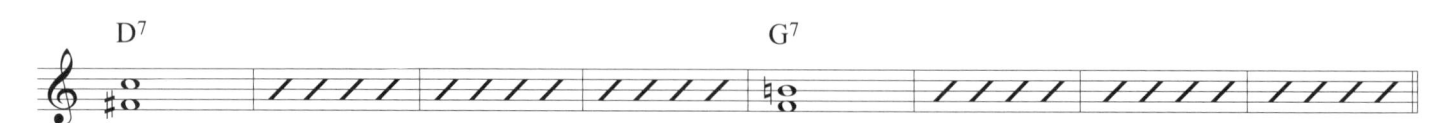

It would be worth taking some rehearsal time to teach this to the group. Ask them to sing the roots while the rhythm section plays through the sequence. Get them to sing the words 'one', 'four' and 'five' in the appropriate places. If they have difficulty in hearing the root progression, split the ensemble up and have some play the roots, as a guide, while everyone else sings. Always bear in mind that the purpose is to instil the harmonic pacing of the sequence into the group.

Once everyone is confident with the roots, break the group up and sing the guide tones as well. Remember that the guide tones are the 3rds and 7ths of the chord types, and they depict the essential qualities of the harmony. Again, once everybody seems confident enough, get the rhythm section to 'tacet' and have the players sing unaccompanied. With just the root notes and the 3rds and 7ths you will have the essence of the harmonic shape. Here is some raw material for soloing. One of the basic and most common resources for soloing is the blues scale.

Example 2: The blues scale

This scale can be superimposed on the whole sequence – it yields interesting sounds and has the added benefit of immediately giving the correct stylistic approach because of the flattened 3rd and 5th. The changing harmony underneath will affect the notes that you play. Sometimes the note will sound very pungent and harsh, at other times just cool.

A close look at the blues scale reveals that it is only a minor pentatonic with one note (the flattened 5th) added, so, for the purposes of this exercise, we can simplify this blues scale still further.

Example 3: Minor pentatonic

54 Bear Cave Blues

Once the basic pattern of both the blues scale and the minor pentatonic have been learnt, it is time to experiment and throw some ideas around. You do not have to play the whole scale; fragments of it will be just as effective. Play the notes in any order. Try starting melodic cells on different notes each time. Here are some examples.

Example 4: Basic blues ideas

Familiarise the students with these raw materials and ask them to practise their own ideas, using only these basic building blocks. A useful 'homework' assignment would be to ask the students to write out two or more of their own blues licks and learn them for use in their solo at the next rehearsal. This idea of working out your ideas in advance may seem to fly in the face of perceived jazz convention, but it is a sure and safe way of developing the language and of building confidence. For a comparison of these basic resources in another setting, see the chapters on *Blue Panther* and *Night Run*.

The blues scale is fun and easily accessible, but there will come a time when the student aspires to the more satisfying aim of creating a solo that reflects the subtleties of the harmonic sequence. This really means observing the shape of the sequence, particularly in its primary movements to the subdominant, the dominant and back to the tonic. In order to do this you will have to understand the guide tones of the sequence and the scale resources of the chords.

The guide tones are shown by hollow noteheads in the following music examples. These are the crucial 3rds and 7ths of the chords involved and, when emphasised, help to represent the crucial corners in the sequence. These guide tones should be thoroughly learnt, so that the notes themselves, and their characteristic sound, are ingrained in the student's musical consciousness. Once the guide tones have been thoroughly assimilated we can move on to the scale to chord theory. As we have seen in previous chapters, the scale resource for the dominant chord shape is the Mixolydian mode. This is the 5th mode of the major scale.

Example 5: Mixolydian scale for I

Example 6: Mixolydian scale for IV

Example 7: Mixolydian scale for V

Notice that each one is related to a specific key. They all have certain notes in common and certain notes that are different. It is the ones that are different that will help you pinpoint the particular chord you are on. Also notice how these Mixolydian modes correspond to the guide tones.

Soloing using just the guide tones and the Mixolydian scales will help depict the tonal movement of the sequence. Limiting yourself to these resources helps you hone the skills you need to navigate a blues sequence successfully, and is well worth the practice and attention.

Example 8: Blues sequence using guide tones and Mixolydian scales

56 Bear Cave Blues

The above example is grammatically correct and musically literate but does not draw heavily on the blues scale, though it has certain blues inflections. Here is a modified version of the solo that uses the blues scale in an idiomatic way, along with guide tones and Mixolydian resources. Compare the two to see how important the blues scale is in setting the mood and how it acts as a contrast to the other devices.

Example 9: Full blues chorus

Blue Panther

Composer: Howard McGill

Solos

This piece has two solo sections, both of which are ideally suited to the novice improviser, with the simpler of the two solo sections acting as a good training ground, or dry run, for the main solo section. This solo section, therefore, is eminently approachable by musicians with no jazz experience at all. This format allows players to 'dip their toes' before taking the plunge.

Solo Section 2

Purely for reasons of form the 'training' solo section appears in the score as solo section 2, so we will look at this one first. Remember, though, that you are completely at liberty to move this section to wherever you think it works best for your ensemble. In the score you will find this section at letter C. The ensemble have a two-bar 'send off' to set up a two-bar break for the soloist. This happens twice to form an eight-bar open repeat section, giving an opportunity for even the most timid member of the group to solo.

Not only is this solo section brief, but it has other deliberately 'built-in' safety features.
• The solos are always on the one chord (D minor) throughout, so there are no harmonic complications.
• The tempo is an easy medium swing.
• You cannot mess up the form as the ensemble writing punctuates the structure and dictates a call-and-response type format.
• You can use the figures written for the head as starting vocabulary.

Here are some basic ideas from which to construct your improvisations. Firstly, the D blues scale.

Example 1: Blues scale on D

This will provide plenty of scope to find interesting sounds and 'blue' notes. It will also be in everybody's ears, as the melody of the piece is constructed from it.

Example 2: Section of the melody

Try using fragments of the melody to create solos.

Example 3: Melody fragments for creating solos

A good assignment for the class would be to write out a couple of ideas based on the melody and then get them to play them in the rehearsal session with the band. Besides the blues scale there is the simpler option of D minor pentatonic. This five-note pattern will access certain important sounds.

Example 4: D minor pentatonic

If you have studied the performance note on *Bear Cave Blues*, you will already be familiar with the following information. Note that the minor pentatonic is derived from a mode of the major pentatonic, in this case F major pentatonic.

Example 5: F major pentatonic

Also notice that the blues scale is really just a pentatonic with a chromatic approach note to and from the 5th.

Finally there is D Dorian: this is the 2nd mode of the major scale, in this instance the 2nd mode of C major.

Example 6: D Dorian

Note that this includes the notes in the D minor pentatonic but also introduces some new notes to play around with, namely E and B♮. Here are some ideas using Dorian mode.

Example 7: Dorian minor ideas

The best option is of course to combine all three, thereby creating harmonic interest and idiomatic blues inflection, whilst giving yourself the widest possible array of musical resources from which to construct interesting musical ideas.

Example 8: Vocabulary

Solo Section 1

The main solo section is on an AABA form. Fortunately the A sections are all on D minor, which we have just had a significant work-out on. So, all the ideas we have just developed for solo section 2 will work on the A sections of solo section 1. The difference between them is that here in solo section 1 plenty of space is available to develop ideas, use contrasting approaches harmonically, and generally experience more freedom.

On the B section we move to G minor. This is a movement to the subdominant, and very characteristic of the blues. The scale choice given in the score is the Dorian mode, which in this case is the 2nd mode of the F major scale. Do not forget how well the guide tone approach works in describing the harmony. If you aim for the 3rd, which is a B♭, then you will be targeting a defining note for this harmonic change.

Lastly, we should consider the form of this solo section. For novice improvisers the common problem with an AABA form is placing the B section at the right moment. If we put several AABAs together we get:

A A B A A A B A A A B A A A B A.

The problem immediately reveals itself, with many A sections in a row. The most likely scenario with an inexperienced ensemble is that players will lose their place in the A sections, and think that it is time to go to the B section when there is actually another A section to go. The form is easily lost, especially when the A sections are all identical. The solution to this problem is to be very conscious of the top of the form, by which we mean the first A section in the AABA grouping. The director can be very helpful in this regard, by cueing the top each time it comes round, and by indicating the move to the B section.

Brecon Beacon

Composer: Howard McGill

Solos

The main solo section here is at letter C, and consists of an AABA form using two minor tonalities on which to improvise. The A sections are on C minor, and the B section moves a tone down to B♭ minor. The groove is a steady straight-8 feel, allowing the soloist a comfortable space in which to explore the melodic properties of these chords.

There is another opportunity to solo in this piece, and this comes at the very beginning. This introduction can form an open section for a solo from various members of the group, while there are optional backing figures and a launch into the main theme which can be played underneath. Alternatively, you might like to use this section as an interlude at any point in the piece. For example it could break up the AABA structure, forming a freer section before a return to the last section of ensemble writing.

The main solo section

Here are some raw materials to work with. There are two main scale resources for this solo section.

Example 1: C Dorian

Example 2: B♭ Dorian

These are both Dorian mode scales, which is the most common type of minor scale used in jazz. Dorian is the 2nd mode of the major scale, so we can see where these scales are derived from. The Dorian mode on C is the 2nd mode of B♭ major scale, and the Dorian mode on B♭ is the 2nd mode of A♭ major. The scales from which the modes are derived are commonly referred to as the parent scales. Although derived from a simple major scale, each mode has a sound and flavour all its own. Let us take a further look at the particular qualities of the Dorian mode.

As we know, the most obvious thing about Dorian is that it is a minor scale, that is to say it has a flattened 3rd rather than a major 3rd. But what is it that distinguishes it from the many other minor scales that exist? The other two minor scales you are likely to know are harmonic minor and melodic minor. Remember that in jazz theory when we talk about the melodic minor we do so in its ascending form only. As we have already seen, the flattened 6th and 7th in the traditional descending minor melodic just turns the scale into Aeolian mode.

Example 3: C harmonic

Example 4: C melodic

Example 5: C Dorian

Look at the differences between these scales. The harmonic minor has a flattened 6th and a raised 7th, while the ascending melodic minor has a natural 6th and a major 7th. Dorian mode has a natural 6th but a flattened 7th. So the only differences between these scales occur on the 6th and 7th degrees. As the natural 6th and the flattened 7th are the particular characteristics of the Dorian mode, why not bring them out in your improvisation?

Here is some vocabulary to help you do this.

Example 6: Basic vocabulary

The last of these four-bar phrases is the main theme at letter A. The composer has created the phrase out of some interesting intervallic relationships in the mode. The melody leaps from the minor 3rd to the 9th and then descends to that bright sounding natural 6th. The answering phrase then starts on the flat 7th, reiterates the natural 6th and resolves to the 5th. Try making up your own examples.

Ask the players to compose some lines that bring out the characteristics of the Dorian mode, using both C Dorian and then B♭ Dorian. These would be of direct practical use for their soloing as well.

Here are some more examples in B♭ Dorian. These can be used on the B section.

Example 7: Examples on B♭ Dorian

Before becoming an assured improviser a player has to achieve a certain dexterity with the basic melodic properties of the chords. This means learning patterns and motifs, and committing them to memory. Try taking the scale and learning the following basic patterns.

Example 8: Basic patterns

64 Brecon Beacon

There are of course many other scale work-outs you can make up. The object is to give you options and plenty of choice in the scale resource. If you practise all these patterns you will find you can start a phrase on any note and then have the instrumental dexterity to move to anywhere you choose. Soon you will be improvising your own lines and phrases, and mixing up the patterns in a creative way.

Lastly, there is the matter of the form. As we have already seen it is easy to get lost in the form, either by going to the B section too soon or by missing one of the repeated A sections. The backing figures are there to help you find your way. Notice that these figures are rhythmically altered in the B section, and that the B section has a lead-in figure to 'announce' it.

Night Run
Composer: Eddie Harvey

Solos

This is a minor twelve-bar blues in an accessible rock style. You can get by on the soloing on this one with a couple of pentatonics and plenty of blues scale use. The key is D minor, which is the same key as *Blue Panther*. In the chapter on that piece there is a lot of help given in exploring the D minor tonality and D blues scale. All this information will transfer to this piece as well. This will be an interesting exercise for the group to apply the same harmonic knowledge and learned patterns to another style. It will also be greatly encouraging, as it will be an incentive to know that once you have done the work in one key it is transferable to other contexts.

Here is the D blues scale again.

Example 1: D blues scale

And here is the D minor pentatonic on which the blues scale is based.

Example 2: D minor pentatonic

Notice that the chord symbol used is Dm^6. This does not change the function of the chord, but just means that there is a major 6th in the voicing. This is added for colour, and serves no strictly functional purpose. If you have read the chapter on *Brecon Beacon* you will know that a typical scale choice for a minor chord in jazz is the Dorian scale. The Dorian mode is the 2nd degree of the major scale, so in this case D Dorian would be used, which is the 2nd mode of the C major scale.

Brecon Beacon was a good workout on two different Dorian scales and, if you are familiar with this chapter, you will know that an important characteristic of this scale is the natural 6th. Here is the Dorian scale.

Example 3: Dorian scale

To teach the group this scale, ask them all to play C major scale, and then have them start on the 2nd degree, going up and down exactly the same collection of notes.

Make sure they are hearing this as D minor by getting the pianist to play a D minor chord to accompany them. The important thing to remember here is that the D Dorian collection comes from the parent scale of C major.

The next chord is a G^7 chord. This is a move to the subdominant as is typical of blues sequences. In a traditional minor blues one would expect the subdominant to be a minor chord, but here the composer cleverly allows for the same scale resource by keeping the parent scale the same and changing the subdominant chord to a major one.

G^7 is also from the same family of chords as D minor, as it can also be seen as a V^7 chord in C, therefore coming from the same parent scale.

| Dm | G^7 | Cmaj^7 |

This means that again you can use C major scale as a scale resource, only this time starting on the 5th degree, meaning that you use the Mixolydian mode.

Example 4: Mixolydian on G

You will find also that the D minor pentatonic will also work on this chord and the D blues scale, but each will sound different because of its changed musical context.

In bars 7 and 8 of the sequence there is a return to chord I, that is, Dm^6. Thus the entire first eight bars of the twelve-bar sequence can be dealt with using the same melodic properties, namely the Dorian and Mixolydian modes drawn from the same parent scale, C major.

Having given the soloist such an easy ride for the first eight bars, the composer poses a few problems in the next four. What we have here is a modified minor II–V–I. A minor II–V–I is actually quite hard to negotiate for a beginner, requiring a different scale resource for each chord and a knowledge of chromatic extensions on dominants.

Because of this the composer has simplified the II chord and the V chord to make sure that they have similar scale resources, thus making the sequence easier to solo over. For rehearsal purposes you might consider looping the last four bars of the sequence to let everybody have a concentrated go at negotiating this cadence. Scale choices are given in the score and parts, and here we provide several examples to start the ball rolling.

Example 5: II-V-I examples

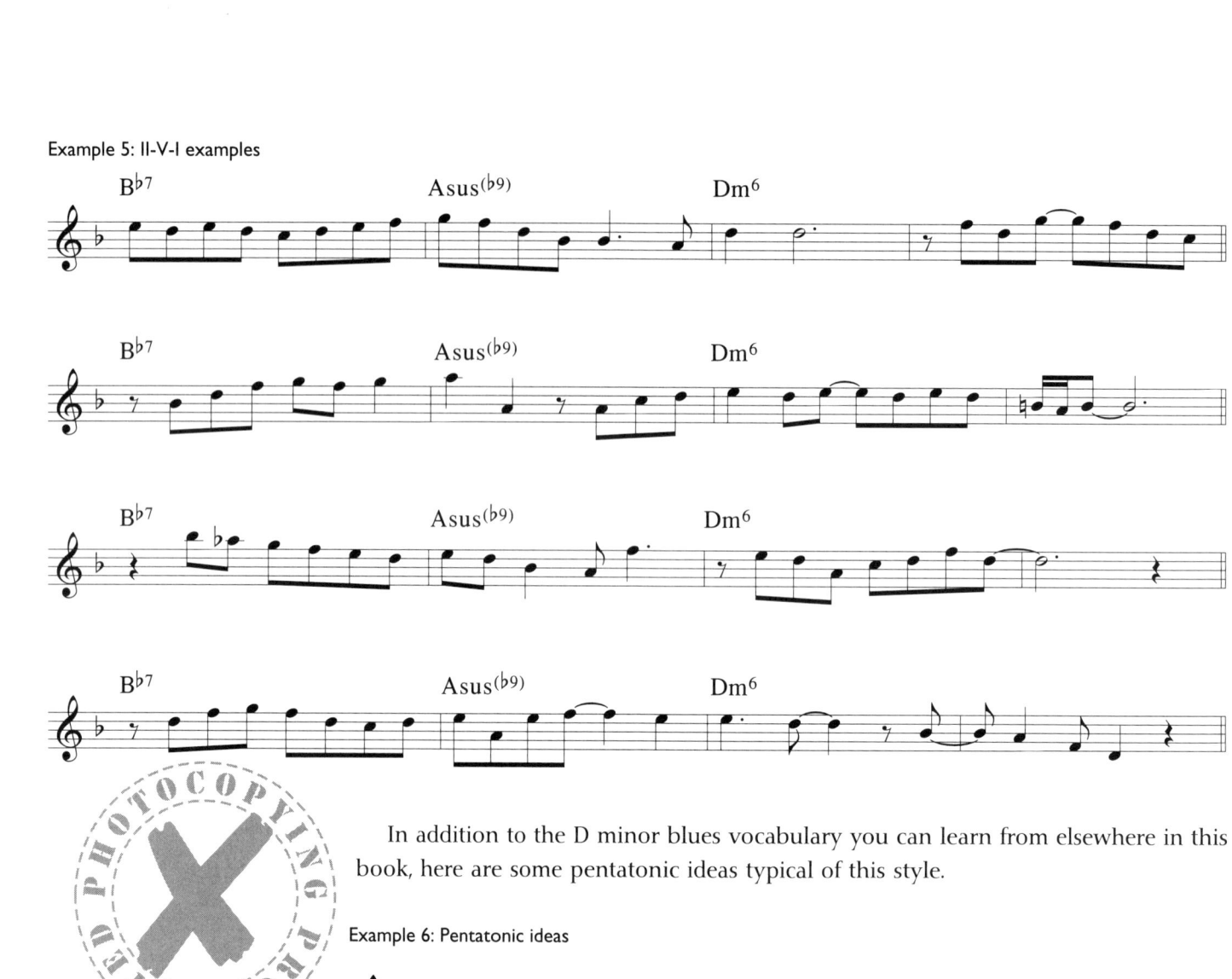

In addition to the D minor blues vocabulary you can learn from elsewhere in this book, here are some pentatonic ideas typical of this style.

Example 6: Pentatonic ideas

68 Night Run

Slice and Dice

Composer: John Warren

Solos

There are in effect three solo sections. The first one, at letter G, is based entirely on a chord of G⁷. The second, at letter H, is based on a G pedal point, and the last, at the fifth bar of letter H, is based on a II–V–I to C major. Despite each solo section having seemingly different harmony and chords the scale resource to use on all of them is C major.

More interesting still is that, despite each chord having the same scale resource, each solo section will sound very different, making the piece a rewarding musical experience.

Solo Section 1

This section is all based on G⁷. Remember that if a dominant shape is being used over a root note that sounds like chord I (or the 'tonic' to use its classical equivalent) which is the case here, it is likely to sound very bluesey. Consequently it is appropriate to use the G blues scale here.

Example 1: G blues scale

Here also is the pentatonic that the blues scale is derived from.

Example 2: G pentatonic

You may be wondering why the B♭ works against a G⁷ voicing, which clearly contains a B♮. This is because the B♭ acts as a sharpened 9th chromatic extension. It is the clash with the B♮ which gives it that pungent and dissonant quality which, when you get used to it, does not sound harsh, just funky!

From an educational point of view, however, this piece has been devised as a way of introducing the II–V–I cadence. It is therefore probably best to encourage soloing on the Mixolydian mode, as this scale will transfer to apply to all the other chords in the piece. Here is the Mixolydian scale starting on G which in this case is the 5th mode of C major.

Example 3: G Mixolydian

As with the Dorian mode we have looked at in other chapters, you should aim to discover the particular melodic characteristics of this mode, and encourage soloists to bring them out in their improvisations. All modes are distinct sounds in their own right, and not necessarily simply inversions of their parent scales. The Mixolydian mode is distinct in that it is a major scale but does not have a leading note, unlike the ordinary major scale that you are very familiar with. There is, in fact, a tone rather than a semitone between the 7th degree and the tonic. This is the only thing that distinguishes it from the common major scale (which incidentally is called Ionian mode). Here are some examples of what works on G^7, using the Mixolydian mode.

Example 4: G^7 in Mixolydian mode

Solo Section 2a

The chordal accompaniment is more colourful here, but functionally the same. We still have a G pedal point, essentially creating a dominant on G. However, the sequence does actually sound quite different from the previous one. This is because the new chords the composer introduces access some colourful extensions above the basic chord of G^7.

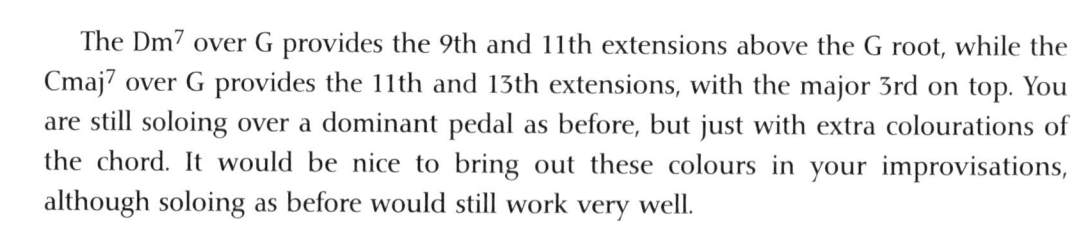

The Dm^7 over G provides the 9th and 11th extensions above the G root, while the $Cmaj^7$ over G provides the 11th and 13th extensions, with the major 3rd on top. You are still soloing over a dominant pedal as before, but just with extra colourations of the chord. It would be nice to bring out these colours in your improvisations, although soloing as before would still work very well.

Try the following ideas as a starting point. Note that they either start on, or emphasise, the extensions above the chords, and that they use arpeggiated figures.

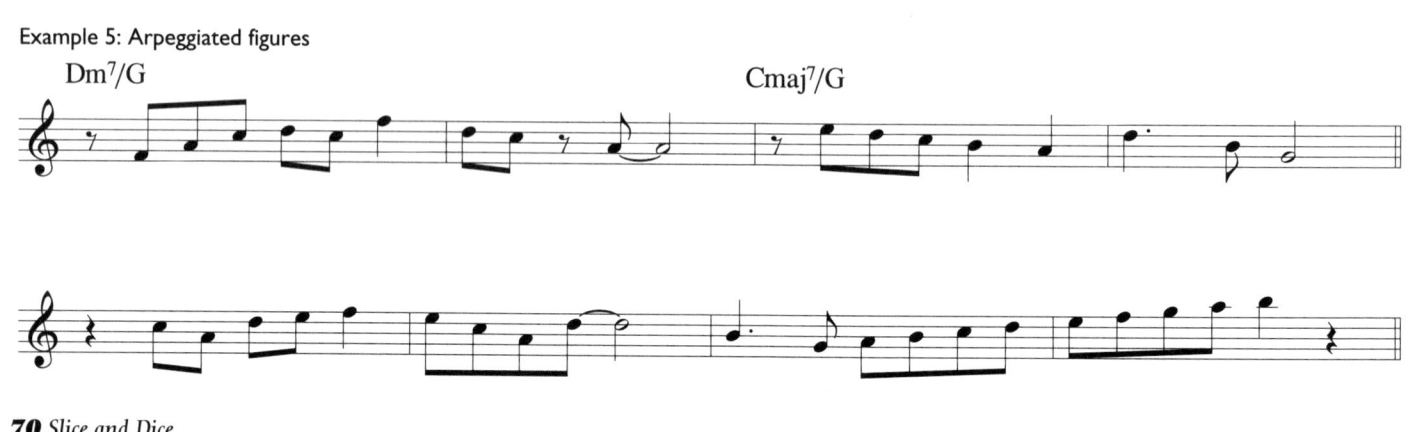

Example 5: Arpeggiated figures

Dm^7/G $Cmaj^7/G$

If you ever needed ammunition to convince your pupils of the value of practising scales and arpeggios, here it is.

Solo Section 2b

Now we finally get the full II–V–I cadence. This sequence will again feel different from the others, as it will have a definite feeling of resolution. This type of cadence is one of the main building blocks on which many jazz chord sequences are built. Dm is chord II of C major, G^7 is chord V, and the resolution is to chord I, $Cmaj^7$. As all three chords are derived from each other, the scale resource is the same for all three. For a fuller explanation of the II–V–I refer to the relevant section on jazz conventions.

Although you can use the same scale over the entire chord sequence, it will be a lot more satisfying to hear each chord being dealt with in its own right. That is to say that the soloist has to make the Dm chord sound like chord II, the G^7 chord sound like the dominant, and the $Cmaj^7$ chord sound like the resolution to the tonic. One way to do this is to bring out the guide tones.

Example 6: Guide tones

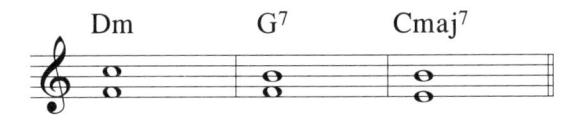

This will help bring out the horizontal movement of the sequence. Here are some examples of how to create a line that does this.

Example 7: Horizontal movement

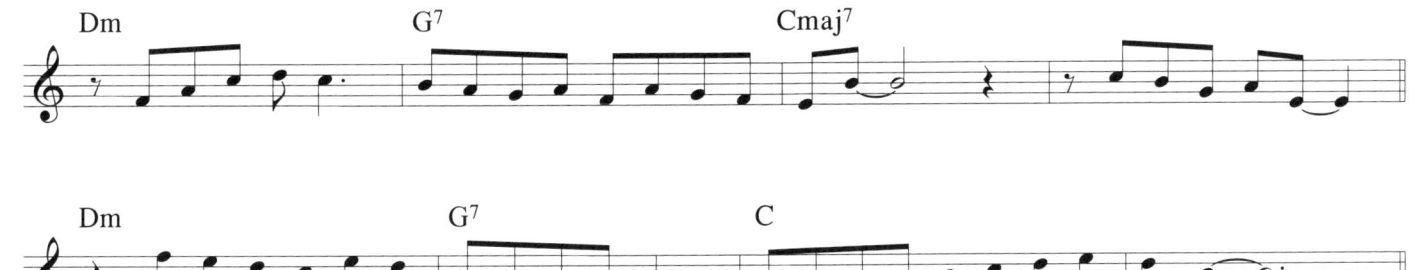

You can also try arpeggiating the chords, so that the harmonic shapes are described by the melodic line.

Example 8: Arpeggiating chords

In conclusion, this piece provides a good workout in the key of C, and two other chords, namely chord II and chord V, that help to define it. The II–V–I is so important in the construction of jazz chord sequences that it has to be addressed extensively by all jazz musicians.

Straw Boss

Composer: Jeremy Price

Solos

This is a twelve-bar blues in C using only the basic dominant chord types. As well as individual soloing there is scope for group improvisation in the form of making up backing riffs, alternative heads and shout choruses. You can, of course, use the C blues scale as a melodic resource to improvise with. A more rewarding solo will be created by making use of guide tones and the appropriate Mixolydian scales as well.

The part writing deliberately outlines the harmonic changes and provides a starting point for vocabulary. So this piece should provide an ideal vehicle for young or inexperienced players, giving them the opportunity to do some thorough ground work on this fundamental form for jazz improvisation.

Because of the way the melody is constructed it might be profitable to start by looking at the guide tones.

The guide tones, as explained in the chapter on jazz conventions, are really just a means of plotting the horizontal movement through the harmonic sequence. They are usually the 3rds and 7ths of the chord, as these notes are very important in describing what type of chord it is. They also very often pinpoint crucial notes that are different from the previous chord.

In order to describe or represent the harmonic movement in the improvised line it is necessary to understand and be able to use these important notes. Notice that the head at letter A is a repeated rhythmic figure based on an ascending line. The top note of each line is one of the guide tones to the harmony. Compare this chart of the guide tones to the head at letter A.

Example 1: Guide tones

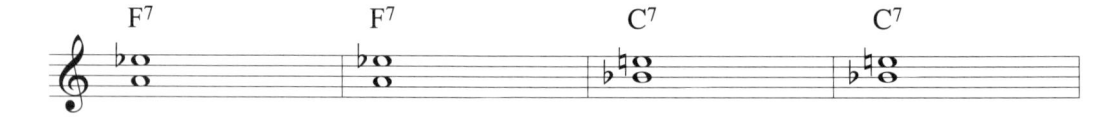

Notice how the head mirrors the guide tone root. Also, look at the accompanying backing figures to the head and see how these also follow the guide tones, whilst also bringing out the rhythmic qualities of the melody.

So, as you can see, the head and the backing figures at letter A have been deliberately written as an aid to teaching the guide tones.

As discussed in earlier chapters, the blues scale is an accessible resource for the beginner, allowing stylistic and idiomatic playing without requiring much knowledge or instrumental dexterity. However, the blues is a twelve-bar format with a beginning, middle and end that the more mature improviser will find satisfying to address. This twelve-bar format can be seen as three lots of four-bar units.

The first four bars are a statement of the home key, reinforced by a brief departure to the subdominant in the second bar only to swiftly return again for bars 3 and 4. The second four bars show a more significant move to the subdominant, again returning to the home key for the last two bars. The third and final set of four bars starts on the dominant and descends to the tonic via the subdominant, forming a V–IV–I cadence. Then the dominant is restated to prepare for a return to the top of the sequence.

Each four bars is distinctly different and has a functional role in giving harmonic shape to the twelve-bar sequence. The soloist should address this shape, making it clear through the choice of notes whether he or she is on the tonic, subdominant or dominant. This is done by targeting the guide tones and using the appropriate Mixolydian scale.

Here are the three Mixolydian scales you will need. Remember that the Mixolydian scale is the 5th mode of the major scale and notice that the 3rd and 7th of each scale are also the guide tones.

Example 2: Three Mixolydian scales

This is not to say that use of the blues scale should be eventually ruled out, but rather that the blues inflections should be interwoven in and around the harmonic detail.

The following example is a complete chorus of a blues solo. See if you can see where the blues scale is used and where the melodic line manages to arrive on the crucial guide tones just at the right moment. Also see how the Mixolydian scales make a nice change from the blues scale sound, and how they seem to represent the harmonic detail more effectively.

Example 3: Blues solo chorus

There are lots of different riffs written to accompany the solos. Some are blues-based and essentially rhythmic, while others follow the guide tones. These can all be used as starting points for acquiring improvising vocabulary. Take one of the ideas, either in total or just as a fragment. See what can be done with the basic shell by modifying it rhythmically or in pitch. Think about what you like about the phrase and why you think it works, and then incorporate the same properties in other melodic lines.

The last solo section starts with a bass solo. This is deliberately directed so that the dynamic of the whole piece comes right down, providing a place to build from towards the end. After the bass solo try introducing another front line soloist, perhaps with just a walking bass accompaniment. Add the other rhythm-section members one by one, cue some backings then eventually return to the head.

Glossary

Introduction

One of the best ways to understand jazz is to strip it down to its constituent parts, thereby gaining an understanding of how they work, before putting them back together again.

As we strip the pieces down to their basic building blocks we have to 'name the parts'. Whilst we have tried to respect the plurality of jazz in all its multi-cultural guises, we have had to settle on a working vocabulary. You will find explanations for all terms used in this glossary, along with other common equivalents. For example, the 'middle eight' is a well-known term – it describes the B section of an AABA form. However, many musicians refer to this as 'the bridge'.

When it comes to chord naming we enter very troubled waters. Many systems and hybrids of systems abound, generally creating a sense of confusion and alienation amongst inexperienced jazz musicians. We have taken the most logical educational approach in standardising our chord names so that, where possible, the chord name as it appears on the score and parts 'explains' itself. So, we do not use a circle for a diminished chord, we use the suffix 'dim'. Likewise we do not use the standard 'half diminished' symbol (a circle with a diagonal line through it); instead we prefer the more long-winded, but ultimately more self-explanatory, 'm$^{7(\flat 5)}$'. This symbol explains that the chord is merely a minor 7th with a lowered 5th, and it is possible to work this out from the chord name. Other ways of 'spelling' this chord (such as a circle with a line through it) will be encountered in jazz notation and these must also be learnt and understood. The system employed in Jazz Works has been adopted because it is the most appropriate to the nature and purpose of the series.

If you are in any doubt about any technical terms used just refer to this glossary or the section on chord symbols on page 77. As well as explaining what the terms mean, we give common equivalents.

Glossary of terms

B section: the third section of an AABA form. Usually this section moves away from the home key that has been established and affirmed in the A sections, setting up a return to it for the final A section. The standard AABA form in jazz is 32 bars long, with each section lasting eight bars. For this reason the B section has also come to be known as the middle eight. It is also sometimes referred to as the 'bridge', as it bridges the gap between the A sections.
Backbeat: the alternate beats in a bar, typically beats 2 and 4 in common time.
Backing figure: melodic fragments played by the rest of the ensemble behind a solo. These can be written out or improvised collectively.

Blowing: improvising (any instrument, even rhythm section).

Bridge: see 'B section'.

Changes: chord sequence.

Comp: accompanying.

Cue: the act of signalling to the musicians that an event is about to take place.

Dominant: the chord type that takes a flattened 7th, but that does not necessarily function as a dominant 7th in the strictest sense.

Ensemble: This has two meanings: 1) the ensemble section – a composed section of the piece in which the ensemble as a whole features, or 2) ensemble playing – referring to how the players work together as an ensemble.

Form: this can mean either the form of the piece as a whole (intro, head, interlude, etc.) or the form of the head (AABA). Phrases like 'soloing on the form' or 'pointing up the form' refer to the second meaning.

Front line: players other than the rhythm section.

Groove: a combination of the style and feel of the piece, e.g. Swing, Latin, Rock, etc.

Guide tones: the important 'descriptive notes in a chord'. Usually the 3rd and 7th, though not always.

Head: main melody.

Inner dynamics: light and shade (both rhythmic and dynamic) within a melody.

Interlude: a composed section of music that can be used anywhere in the piece, though usually to break up solos or to form a link between other sections in the piece.

Intro: introduction.

Kicks: rhythmic accents within general comping.

Lick: a prepared phrase used by a soloist when improvising.

Middle eight: see 'B section'.

Mode: type of scale with a distinct arrangement of tones and semitones.

Open: a section that can be repeated as many times as you like.

Progression: series of chords within a chord sequence, or the entire chord sequence.

Pushes: accented rhythmic syncopations.

Rhythm section: piano, bass, drums and guitar.

Riff: a melodic fragment used either as the basis for musical development or as a backing figure behind a soloist.

Scale: a collection of notes following a pre-determined pattern.

Scale resource: a written-out collection of notes to be used as a basic resource when improvising a solo.

Solo: in this book used as a verb (to solo, soloing) or noun (the solo).

Turnaround: a short chord progression that brings the harmony back to (and thereby affirms) the home key.

Voicing(s): the way a chord is played, with particular reference to the intervals between the notes of the chords. It can relate to piano, guitar, or the ensemble.

Chord Chart

Here is a selection of some of the most common chord types to be found in jazz music. For the purposes of these examples, all the chords are based on the root of C and voiced for piano. Where appropriate, common alternative chord names are included.

PHOTOCOPYING PROHIBITED

Major	Minor	Diminished 7th
C	Cm or C-	Cdim^7 or C^{o7}

Major 7th	Minor 7th	Augmented
Cmaj^7 or C$^\Delta$	Cm^7 or C-^{7}	Caug or C+

Major 9th	Minor 9th	7th, sharpened 9th
Cmaj^9 or C$^{\Delta 9}$	Cm^9 or C-^{9}	C$^{7(\sharp 9)}$

Major 7th, sharpened 11th	Sus 4	7th, sharpened 11th
Cmaj$^{7(\sharp 11)}$ or C$^{\Delta 7(\sharp 11)}$	Csus^4 or Csus	C$^{7(\sharp 11)}$

7th	Minor 7th, flattened 5th (also called half diminished)	6-9
C^7	Cm$^{7(\flat 5)}$ or C$^{\o}$	C$^{6/9}$

9th	Diminished	F over C
C^9	Cdim or C^o	F/C

11th		B$\flat$ over C
C^{11}		B$\flat$/C

For more information on chromatically extended dominants and altered chords, see the relevant sections of the advanced level Teacher's Book.

Discography

The following is neither representative nor exhaustive, but it will give you a starting point for your listening. Some of the recordings are 'landmarks', while others have been selected because they represent a general style or a particular artist. Where appropriate we have flagged links between the recommended listening and pieces in Jazz Works. For example, as *Art's Groove* (initial level) is a homage to Art Blakey, Blakey recordings have been recommended in relation to this piece. Otherwise we have given the recordings a general reference, either by instrument or to an aspect of jazz ensemble playing such as rhythm section work, for example.

Artist	Album	Label (original in brackets)	No.	Reference
Cannonball Adderley	Something Else	Blue Note	0777 7 4630826	alto saxophone
Nat Adderley	Work Song	Original Jazz Classic (Riverside)	OJC203632	cornet
Arild Andersen	Sagn	ECM	849 647-2	double bass
Louis Armstrong	Hot 5 & Hot 7	Giants of Jazz	CD53001	trumpet/cornet
Chet Baker	Chet	Original Jazz Classic (Riverside)	OJC20 087-2	trumpet/flugel
Chet Baker	Chet Baker Plays the Best of Lerner & Loewe	Original Jazz Classic (Prestige)	OJCCD 137-2	trumpet/flugel
Count Basie	On The Road	Original Jazz Classic (Pablo)	OJCCD 854-2	*Straw Boss*
Count Basie	Live In Japan '78	Pablo	CD2308 246	*Straw Boss*
Count Basie	Fun Time	Pablo	CD2310 945	*Straw Boss*
Art Blakey	The Best of Art Blakey	Blue Note	93205 2	drums/*Art's Groove*
Art Blakey	Caravan	Original Jazz Classic (Riverside)	OJCCD 038-2	drums/*Art's Groove*
Art Blakey	Kyoto	Original Jazz Classic (Riverside)	OJCCD 145-2	*Art's Groove*
Ron Carter	New York Slick	Original Jazz Classic (Milestones)	OJCCD 916-2	double bass
Chick Corea	Now He Sings, Now He Sobs	Blue Note	CDP7 90055 2	piano
Chick Corea	Trio Music	ECM	827 702-2	piano
Miles Davis	Sketches of Spain	CBS	4606042	trumpet
Miles Davis	58 Sessions, featuring Stella by Starlight	Columbia Jazz	4679182	trumpet
Duke Ellington	The Ellington Suites	Original Jazz Classic (Pablo)	OJCCD 446-2	piano/composition/ensemble playing
Stan Getz	Quartets	Original Jazz Classic (Prestige)	OJCCD 121-2	tenor saxophone
Herbie Hancock	Speak Like A Child	Blue Note	CDP 7461362	piano
Art Pepper	Modern Jazz Classics	Original Jazz Classic (Contemporary)	OJCCD 341-2	saxophones
John Warren	The Brass Project	ECM	518 362-2	*Slice and Dice*
Kenny Wheeler	Gnu High	ECM	825 591-2	trumpet/flugel

On the CD

This CD was recorded live so as to create the sense that a performance was happening in real time, with real musicians interacting with each other. It is not supposed to be a carefully manicured commercial recording, but a representation of what a group of musicians made of the pieces on a certain day. These are not definitive performances and should not be copied. They are an illustration of what the pieces might sound like given a certain interpretation. We recorded several versions of each piece and decided which version to use on the CD by the quality of the improvised solos, not by the quality of, for example, the ensemble playing taken as a whole. The standard of some solos is above the general initial level standard.

Band 1 - Steve Waterman, trumpet & flugel horn; Mike Williams, alto saxophone/flute; Julian Siegel, tenor & baritone saxophones/clarinet; Jeremy Price, trombone; Simon Purcell, piano; Andy Jones, guitar; Tim Wells, bass; Tom Gordon, drums.

Band 2 - Steve Waterman, trumpet; Mike Williams, alto saxophone/flute; Julian Siegel, tenor & baritone saxophones/clarinet; Jeremy Price, trombone; Simon Purcell, piano; Andy Jones, guitar; Phil Mulford, bass; Tom Gordon, drums.

Notes on the performances

During the sessions the players decided to amend the pieces, with the following results. On *Brecon Beacon* they decided to put in a four-bar repeat at bars 69-72 (i.e. they played the preceding four bars again). On *Night Run* they inserted a 16-bar section before the recap of the head to allow the bass player to have a solo. On *Slice and Dice* they chose to play coda 1, but instead of a true 'repeat and fade' end, they agreed to improvise an ending when it felt right to do so.

Track No.	Title & Composer	Band No.	Front line instrumentation	Solos
1	Art's Groove (Frank Griffith)	1	trumpet, alto saxophone, tenor saxophone, trombone	Andy Jones (guitar), Mike Williams (alto saxophone)
2	Azul (Mike Sheppard)	2	trumpet, alto saxophone, tenor saxophone, trombone	Simon Purcell (piano), Jeremy Price (trombone)
3	Bear Cave Blues (Malcolm Miles)	1	trumpet, alto saxophone, tenor saxophone, trombone	Simon Purcell (piano), Jeremy Price (trombone)
4	Blue Panther (Howard McGill)	1	clarinet, trumpet, alto saxophone, trombone	Julian Siegel (clarinet), Steve Waterman (trumpet), Mike Williams (alto saxophone), Jeremy Price (trombone)
5	Brecon Beacon (Howard McGill)	1	soprano saxophone, flugel horn, alto saxophone, trombone (with cup mute)	Steve Waterman (flugel horn), Julian Siegel (soprano saxophone)
6	Night Run (Eddie Harvey)	2	trumpet, trombone (on part 2), alto saxophone, baritone saxophone (on part 4)	Steve Waterman (trumpet), Andy Jones (guitar), Phil Mulford (electric bass)
7	Slice and Dice (John Warren)	1	trumpet, alto saxophone, tenor saxophone, trombone	Andy Jones (guitar), Jeremy Price (trombone), Mike Williams (alto saxophone), Julian Siegel (tenor saxophone)
8	Straw Boss (Jeremy Price)	1	flute, trumpet (muted), baritone saxophone, trombone (muted)	Mike Williams (flute), Jeremy Price (trombone), Tim Wells (bass)

Index

A section 46, 48, 49, 50, 52
AABA form 22, 46, 50, 60, 61, 62
Accents 29, 33
Aeolian (mode/scale) 52, 63
African township 7
Answering phrase 43
Art's Groove 46
Articulation 30, 31, 32
Azul 50

B section 22, 26, 47, 49, 52
Backing riffs 72
Backings (backing figures) 15, 20, 21, 23, 44, 50, 62, 65, 73, 74
Basic ride pattern 33
Bass 33, 34
Bass drum 34
Bass lines 26
Bear Cave Blues 53, 59
Beat 17, 20
Bends 29
'Blue' notes 58
Blue Panther 55, 58, 66
Blues inflection 60, 73
Blues licks 55
Blues scale 6, 12, 42, 46, 47, 49, 54, 55, 57, 58, 59, 66, 67, 69, 72, 73, 74
Blues sequence 56, 67
Breath support 31
Breathing 18
Brecon Beacon 62, 66

Cadences 12, 40, 41, 67
Cadential progression 44
Call-and-response 13, 46, 58
Chord changes 26, 39, 42, 53
Chord notation 26
Chord progression 43
Chord sequence 39, 47, 50, 71
Chord symbols 12, 13, 16, 26, 36, 37, 38
Chord types 50, 72
Chord voicings 15
Chords 5, 25, 26, 39, 56, 58, 64, 69
Chorus 15, 20, 21, 74
Chromatic alterations 37
Chromatic approach chords 44
Chromatic extensions 48, 67, 69
Chromatic passing notes 49
Codas 16, 20
Comping 15
Composer 5, 37
Compound time 33, 34, 35
Conductor 17
'Corners' 13, 50, 52, 55
Counter-themes 15
Count-ins 18, 19, 20
Cues (cueing) 16, 20, 21, 23, 61

Davis, Miles 7
Debussy, Claude 39, 41, 42
Dexterity 43
Diatonic harmony 39
Directions 20, 21, 24
Director 17, 20, 22, 61
Dominant chord types 50, 51
Dominant 7th chord 37
Dorian (mode/scale) 38, 51, 52, 59, 60, 61, 62, 63, 66, 67, 70
Dorsey, Tommy 17
Downbeat 18, 21, 22
Drums 33
Dynamic swells 31
Dynamics 15, 29, 30, 31, 32, 74

Emphasis 30
Endings 16
Enharmonic re-spellings 36
Ensemble 54, 58, 61
Ensemble chorus 23
Ensemble section 15, 17, 19, 21, 29, 32, 35
Equipment 14
Extensions 44, 70

Feedback session 28
Feel 15, 18, 29, 35
Figured bass 36
Fills 15
V–IV–I cadence 73
Form 13, 15, 16, 17, 20, 21, 22, 23, 25, 26, 27, 28, 34, 42, 50, 58, 61, 65
IV–V–I cadence 41
Foxtrot 17
Front line 14, 23, 26, 29, 30, 31, 34
Functional tonality 36, 41

Garbarek, Jan 7
Goodman, Benny 17
Groove 13, 15, 17, 18, 20, 29, 30, 32, 33, 35, 62
Guide tones 6, 26, 39, 40, 42, 44, 47, 52, 54, 55, 56, 57, 61, 71, 72, 73, 74
Guitar 33, 34

Hancock, Herbie 50
Harmonic changes 72
Harmonic detail 74
Harmonic minor 62, 63
Harmonic movement 39, 40, 42, 52
Harmonic progression 42
Harmonic sequence 55, 72
Harmonic shape 71, 73
Harmony 6, 13, 14, 15, 16, 25, 29, 30, 34, 36, 37, 39, 41, 42, 47, 50, 54, 61, 66, 69, 72
Head 16, 30, 44, 58, 72, 73, 74
Herman, Woody 17
Hi-hat 34
Horizontal movement 72

Improvisation 4, 11, 21, 25, 26, 27, 33, 36, 41, 42, 43, 48, 58, 62, 70, 72
Improviser 39, 42, 49, 61, 64, 73
Inner dynamics 29, 30
Instrumental dexterity 64, 73
Instrumental techniques 29, 30
Instrumentation 14
Interjections 34
Interlude 16, 20, 23, 62
Interpretation 29
Intervallic relationship 63
Introduction 16
Inversions 70
Ionian (mode/scale) 70

James, Harry 17
Jarrett, Keith 7

Köln Concert 7

Latin 18, 19
Launch 62
Licks 11, 42, 43, 44
Linear movement 40
Live performances 25, 35, 42
Long notes 30, 31, 32
Lydian (mode/scale) 48, 49

Maiden Voyage 50
Major 7th chord 36, 37
Melodic cell 43, 54
Melodic characteristics 70
Melodic colour 46
Melodic fragment 44, 51
Melodic ideas 44
Melodic line 29, 42, 47, 52, 71, 74
Melodic minor 62, 63
Melodic properties 26, 27, 28, 36, 40, 62, 64, 67
Melodic resources 25, 27, 28, 37, 40, 42, 72
Melody 25, 59
Minor pentatonic 54, 59, 60, 66, 67
Minor 7th chord 38
Mixolydian (mode/scale) 26, 27, 38, 39, 48, 49, 51, 52, 55, 56, 57, 67, 69, 70, 72, 73, 74
Modes 11, 44, 70
Mood 18
Motifs 48, 64

Naming styles 5
Navigation 24
New section 22, 23
Night Run 55, 66
Non-functional tonality 36
Notation 6, 33, 36

Offbeat 30, 34
Offbeat accents 35
Onbeat 33
Open section 21, 22
Orchestra 17, 20

Parallel movement 47
Parent scale 52, 62, 67
Parts 26, 27, 49, 67
Passing notes 29, 30, 51, 52
Pattern 27, 29, 64, 66
Pentatonic(s) 66, 68, 69
Performance 17, 23, 24
Personnel 14
Phrases 12, 29, 46, 63, 74
Phrasing 17, 29, 30, 35
Piano 33, 34
Pitch 6, 74
Preparation 28
Pulse 18, 20, 29, 33
Pushes 18

Quaver subdivision 29

Recordings 6, 11, 25, 35, 42
Rehearsal 14, 17, 19, 23, 24, 25, 26, 28, 29, 47, 54
'Repeat till ready' fill 44
Rhythm 6, 13, 18, 25, 29, 30, 31, 32, 42, 46
Rhythm section 13, 15, 16, 17, 18, 20, 25, 26, 27, 28, 29, 31, 33, 34, 35, 47, 54, 74
Rhythmic augmentation 53
Rhythmic figure 72
Rhythmic ideas 34
Rhythmic patterns 27, 33
Rhythmic qualities 73
Rhythmic repetition 43
Rhythmic vocabulary 35
Riff 12, 44, 74
Rock 18, 19, 42, 66
Rollins, Sonny 7
Root movement 41, 44, 52, 53
Root notes 54, 69

Root progression 54
Roots 26, 54
Satie, Erik 39
Scale choices 6, 12, 13, 47, 49, 66, 67
Scale options 53
Scale resources 26, 27, 28, 38, 39, 42, 47, 48, 49, 50, 51, 52, 52, 55, 62, 64, 67, 69, 71
Scale to chord theory 26, 36, 51, 55
Scales 5, 11, 16, 27, 36, 48
Score 25, 26, 27, 49, 58, 67
Sequence 16, 22, 25, 26, 27, 28, 34, 39, 53, 54, 55, 56, 67, 70, 71, 73
Shorter, Wayne 50
Shout chorus 72
Signals 20, 21, 22, 23, 24
Slice and Dice 27, 29, 30, 44, 69
Slide vibrato 31
Snare drum 34
Solo section 15, 16, 20, 21, 25, 44, 58, 61, 62
Soloing (soloists) 15, 16, 17, 20, 21, 22, 23, 27, 28, 34, 39, 42, 44, 47, 48, 49, 50, 52, 53, 54, 55, 56, 62, 63, 66, 67, 69, 70, 71, 72
Speech 11
Stamina 18
Stopping 23, 24
Straight quavers 19, 33, 34, 35
Straight 8 19, 62
Stravinsky, Igor 39
Straw Boss 44, 72
Stress 33
Style 15, 17, 18, 20, 25, 29, 31
Stylistic inflection 46
Sus chords 38, 50, 51, 52
Swing 18, 33, 35
Swing quavers 30, 33
Syncopated quaver 34
Syncopation 18, 30, 31, 33

Tempo 15, 17, 18, 19, 20, 58
Theme 14, 15
Theory 13
Tonal area 44
Tonal centre 34, 39, 47, 51
Tonal movement 56
Tonality 36, 42, 50, 62, 66
Tongue stops 31, 32
Transcriptions 6, 11
Transposition 43
Triple time 33, 35
Tritone substitutions 44
Turnarounds 44
Twelve-bar blues 6, 41, 53, 66, 72, 73
Twelve-bar sequence 67
II–V–I cadence 39, 44, 47, 67, 69, 71

Vamp 44
Vibrato 30, 31, 32
Vocabulary 6, 12, 13, 25, 42, 43, 44, 46, 51, 52, 58, 68, 72, 74
Voice leadings 26, 29, 36, 40, 41
Voicings 26, 37

Walking bass line 34, 74
Warren, John 27, 29
West Coast blues 7
Wind band 17, 20

Yes or No 50